Sometimes Daddies Cry

...What a Dad Really Feels

About Divorce

Table of Contents

For Morgan

With Love From Your Daddy

Foreword

I am a dad. It's the only self-definition I have ever cared about in my life. It's the only job I really wanted to be great at. I've always been a hard worker and always risen to the top in my employment endeavors so being defined by my job and how well I perform in it means little to me.

But being a dad was and is the one thing I really, truly worked at. I read books, I listened to radio programs about it. I prayed, and still pray, daily for the grace and wisdom to be better every day than I was the day before. I simply love being a dad.

In December 1999 I became an ex-husband. Maybe the only thing I wanted to be as much as I want to be a great dad was a great husband. I like to think I was on my way, but things happen. You can't make someone else happy...you can only add to their happiness. They have to be happy to begin with. I learned this the hard way as my heart was ripped from my chest by the ending of my marriage.

The divorce was a rejection...make no mistake about that. It took me years to accept it and realize that I was grieving the marriage not the spouse.

In those first dark days of my post-divorce life, I searched for any kind of resource that would steer me *toward* Jesus and not away from Him. Because the intense pain and shame and hurt and anger was already trying to rip my Faith from me. So I drove to the local Lifeway store and hoped I would find a few books about being a dad in a divorced situation. I hoped to find maybe two or three books about men like me who had walked this terrible road and left me something in the way of a well of wisdom and hope. *I found nothing.*

Not one title, not one author who would address this horrible issue from a Biblical, compassionate, loving perspective. Nothing that would teach the Church how to treat a divorced dad. Nothing to help me with my tears. Had I wanted to read about beating my wife in court, hiding my wealth, or "losing that gut and dating younger women" I could have found a dozen or more titles at the Barnes and Noble.

But there was nothing about how empty my house felt that first day without my wife and daughter. Nothing about crying myself to sleep at night and only sleeping on the couch because I missed my wife being next to me. And certainly nothing about tucking my 18 month old daughter in by telephone as my voice broke and sobs were all I could muster. And nothing that helped me deal honestly with the anger and betrayal I felt toward God. There were no books like that at all.

So I wrote one.

What you hold in your hand here is my journal...it's the roadmap of the path I traveled in my journey to healing and restoration. It's not pretty and it's not neat and tidy and it doesn't have all the answers. But it's honest and that's important to a man in the midst of divorce.

If you are a pastor, reading this to learn how to better minister to a divorced man, please listen closely to my voice in these pages. Because you can learn a lot about how this hurts a father.

If you are a friend or family member of a man in the process of divorce, thank you for caring enough to go to this length. I say to you...just *love* him. You can't fix this...but you can lift some of the weight.

If you are a daddy with a broken heart because of divorce, you have a friend. You are a full-time daddy in a part-time world and it's an adjustment that is very hard to make. You can't turn off your loving heart and turn it back on two weekends from now.

You have a friend, a brother in arms who has been through the firefight of divorce. My contact info is within this book. I am here for you.

To all you men I say this...remember; *You are still the Daddy*.

Preface

How this book came to be

I seldom claim to hear directly and audibly from God, but it has happened on occasion. This book is the result of such a moment. One day I was praying and God moved my heart. He spoke to me and told me that this was His vision for my life. I love to write and I do it fairly well. I was to tell my story and lead other men out of this awful nightmare. Somewhere some man was going to read my testimony of the pain I had been in and the battlefield experiences and he was going to say, with great relief, *"at last someone understands! At last, someone has said what I've carried in my soul for years now! Someone else has been there! Someone else is up there ahead of me on this path! It's so dark that I can't see him but whoever he is, left me this well to drink from and maybe it will refresh my soul enough to survive! There is hope!"* Early one morning in September of 2007, I was on my morning walk. I use this time for prayer and I was asking God about a comment my best friend had made the day before. For about two months prior to this particular morning, it seemed like every time anyone would ask me about Holly, and I answered, they would immediately ask me *"would you take her back if you got the chance?"* Each time I responded *"No"* and told them how ridiculous that was. She is remarried and happy and has had another child with her husband. However, it kept occurring that people would ask me this...and it stopped seeming coincidental. The day before, my friend, Jim Wilson asked me the same question, and I was jolted. I asked him, "*Jim why is everyone asking me that lately? I've faced that question about a half dozen times in the last few weeks! I'm finally over her and everyone asks me that!*" Jim's response was startling. He said, "*I don't know...I didn't ask you, the Lord did, and He is telling me right now that YOU need to answer this question in your heart. I don't know why, but that is His word for you.*" While Jim has very often been the man God uses to speak to me, this time rattled me more than any other time in our friendship. Early the next morning, with those words still echoing in my heart, and grief and sadness heavy on my shoulders I cried out to God. I was walking on the circuit at the little park and I asked "*Lord why does it still hurt so much? Why does this pain feel so fresh and new? I was divorced on December 1, 1999...why does it feel like this morning is December 2, 1999?*" Then I heard the voice of God in my soul. It was unmistakable and it touched me to depths I never knew I had in me. He said, "*Son, I told you about three years ago that you were going to have a ministry among hurting divorced men. Recently I have been dialing that vision in, from blurry to clear. If I had taken away this pain, and if I had healed this hurt, you would have forgotten your calling. You could have already been remarried and perhaps even had more children, but there were things you had to experience because other men need what you have to offer and I couldn't let you forget, for their sakes.*" I had to stop in my tracks and bend over like a runner sucking air. I was sobbing. I couldn't speak for a few minutes, but when I did, all I could say was *"Thank you Lord!"* *"Thank you for showing me that you were there all along in my pain, and you have a plan."* *"Thank you for showing me that you will redeem my sorrow and make something great come from it."* I regained my composure and then He spoke again. He said *"There is more, son"* I listened and God spoke these words to my heart, *"You aren't only suffering for yourself. You also feel the burden of thousands of men who can't or won't open up and talk about it themselves. You weep for them and with them. You tell your story because it is also theirs. Your gift to communicate extends beyond telling your own story to telling all their stories too"* So that morning I told God that if I had to suffer, then let me suffer well and let it help some other man to never come down this path. The ones that do have to traverse this dark valley will find a well that God left them so they can have some relief. They have found a friend. They have found a place where they can feel safe amongst others who have seen the same horrors of battle. That is why I wrote this book...and that is why there are several comparisons to the Vietnam War. One of the common threads amongst Vietnam Vets is the feeling they didn't just fight there, they *survived* that war. Divorce is not something you enter into, complete in a set amount of time, and wrap up like a business deal. You endure it. It happens to you. It's like a train wreck. It squeezes you in new ways each day, like a python content to crush you a little at a time. Only if you are equipped do you survive it. This is my own story of divorce. As such, it's very personal and that bears some explaining. I've had folks read the manuscript and occasionally report some discomfort at certain aspects or the personal nature with which I wrote the book. That was the very point of the undertaking…let me explain. Men don't talk very much. We talk in generalities about that which we enjoy or are comfortable with or expert in. Nevertheless, we don't discuss hurts that easily. That's our nature. In order to get the discussion opened up I had to be transparent and vulnerable. I could have left out the parts where I look like a troll but then I'd just be hiding part of the story and that wouldn't spur anyone on to being honest with themselves and maybe stopping the madness. Therefore, I left it all out there. This book reveals truths about my life that might seem extraneous, but revealing them was necessary if I had any hope of perhaps convincing a guy reading it to look deeper into his own life than he was planning to, and to find his own sources of destruction…hopefully *before* they leap out and attack him. So I held back nothing…or at least very little. By being brutally honest, I allow readers to be brutally honest with themselves. If you want to find the truth, you have to be willing to look *everywhere*. You won't find a load of Bible verses either. I am a Christian and I wrote it from that perspective.

However, I found it easier and more therapeutic to relate the application of said verses rather than just quoting them. Many books do that already. Although in the years since I first wrote this, I earned my Bachelors in Religion and became a certified Life Coach, I did not write this as a Theologian or a Counselor. Rather, I am just a guy who went through a heartbreaking divorce and wrote about it.

I am you.

I hope you find a well of refreshing from which to drink.

Sometimes Daddies Cry

What a dad really feels about divorce

On December 1, 1999 my world was dismantled...

My wife and I divorced that day and nothing has been the same since. Divorce hurts in a thousand ways, but none more than the way it affects my relationship with my daughter. 6 years ago, I wrote a song about how it feels...this is my song...and this is my story.

Tuesday afternoon at 3

That's when my world returns to me

Color blooms where all was gray

I'll see my little girl today

Her Barbie backpack and her ponytail

Brings me a smile, it never fails,

But too soon its time to take her home

And once again I'm all alone...

CHORUS

And sometimes Daddy, has to, look the other way

He does not want to, show you

The sadness on his face

Sometimes the strongest man you've ever known is trembling inside

You might not see his tears

But sometimes Daddy cries

Every other Friday, when,

I pick her up for our weekend

She greets me with a hug and kiss

We catch up on the things I've missed

She's growing faster every day

And I miss so much when she's away

Saturday is just a blur

Time slips away when I'm with her.

Sunday evenings' already here
I try to smile and hide my tears
A full time daddy in a part time world
Is hard on me and my little girl
She thinks I'm ten feet tall
Strongest man she ever saw
I drive the fastest car
I'm Handsome as a movie star

I'm wiser than the wisest man
Yeah she's my biggest fan
She thinks I could touch the sky
So I can't let her see me cry.
I wish it turned out differently
And there was more time for you and me
She hugs me tight and with a kiss
I tell her "you're the one I'm gonna miss"
She says "I know Daddy when we're apart"
"You carry me inside your heart"
I wave goodbye and off she rides
And feel the tears that fill my eyes

I never thought I would be here...

I never wanted to be here, I never thought I would be divorced. I adored my wife, she was the most breathtaking beautiful woman I had ever seen in my life, and I loved her more than words could describe. Still here we were, in fourth Circuit Court, on December 1, 1999, about to end our three-year marriage.

We had a tumultuous time together and as recently as the night before, I told her how much I loved her, and I begged her not to go through with this. Then, I swore that if she did, she would be my enemy for life.

Those were empty words. As soon as she walked into that courtroom, my heart went to my throat and I fought back tears. This was not my enemy; this was the woman I loved. I dreamed dreams for her, worked for her, and together we had a beautiful 18-month-old daughter. She was stunning, I was still very much in love with her, and in a few hours, we wouldn't be married anymore.

It was all ending so soon, it hurt so much, and it didn't seem real. I wanted to run up to her and hold her as tightly as I could and beg her not to go through with it. I wanted to throw myself out the window and end the immense pain I was feeling. I wanted someone to wake me up and tell me this was all a dream. Nothing like that was going to happen on this day. Today was reserved for the death of a dream, and the beginning of a nightmare.

When I took my turn on the stand, I couldn't get halfway through my attorneys questions before the tears commenced. I turned to the judge and told her *"I still love my wife…I don't want this".* When it came time to discuss my precious daughter I wept again. She was being discussed like chattel property and it ripped my heart out. She was not a "minor female child" as those emotionless court filings referred to her, she was my sweet little Morgan Wray, named after my grand mother, and she was never going to be the same again after today. Somehow, no matter what the truth was about the situation, this was all my fault.

By 2pm, we were divorced, and it was over. I walked outside and squinted in the early winter sunlight. It was chilly and the sky was clear and blue. How could such a beautiful day hold so much sadness? How did I get here and how did this happen? I felt shell shocked, as if my emotions were drained out of me and held captive in a vault somewhere, like a soldier who had seen too much war. I was the last guy anyone would ever have guessed would be divorced, yet here I was…broken and battered, bandaged up and shipped back out into a world that had changed before my eyes. I woke up that morning a married father, with a wife and a daughter I loved. Before the sun set, my whole identity was altered forever.

I was about to enter the next chapter of a life in turmoil, and I was soon to discover that I not only had my own shame to deal with, but that of the whole world as well. From this day forward, I would always be an ex-husband. From today on, my daughter would never again know a home with both parents.

Nobody wanted to discuss what had happened to me, and their silence betrayed their discomfort. I found myself surrounded by people who had a preconceived notion of what my divorce felt like. Everyone *thought* they knew how it felt, or what to say. They offered their advice on what should have been done, what strategy I could have used to defeat my wife in court, or how lucky I was to have gotten out in one piece when they knew so many men who didn't survive divorce intact. The truth is they knew nothing at all, about what I was feeling. The problem was they didn't understand… at all. All their ideas and all their assumptions were just that…assumptions. Nobody, especially those within the Church community, understood divorce, particularly from a man's perspective. They claimed to know what the Bible says about getting divorced. However, they never came to understand what it feels to be a divorcee. I think the mindset of the church for decades was that if you showed grace and sympathy you would somehow be giving tacit approval to divorce. Divorce was one of those things that the church approached with the attitude that shame was the best preventative. Like the shame of an unplanned pregnancy, if you attach enough shame to it, it will prevent the majority of occurrences. The problem is that it only adds to the hurt and to the inability of the hurting to heal.

In addition, they were wrong on another count…I did not get out intact. Not by a long shot. On the outside, I may have looked the same, but inside I was deeply wounded in ways I hadn't even realized yet, and no one knew any more than how to piece me together. I needed someone to help me adjust to the devastation and the changes I would experience from now on. I needed a friend in the night and an arm around my shoulder. I needed to be able to cry, but men don't do that very well. So there I was...walking wounded, ashamed, defeated. On the outside, I looked the same. I had the same job, lived in the same house, and wore the same clothes. I didn't start dating 24 year olds that weekend, and I didn't forget about my little girl. The only outward signs were the absence of my smile and the vacant hollowness in my eyes. Inside, there was very little left that resembled the man who walked into that Nashville courtroom on that winter morning. What had happened to me, and what *would* happen to me? Was I going to live or just survive? I was so broken hearted, I was just going through the motions, and I was a shell. I had become a ghost, just a ghost. I missed my wife so much I could not find words. So eventually, I stopped trying to find them, and just remained silent. I was bitter, angry, displaced, hurting, and lost. I never intended to be here and I felt so alone and so ashamed and so isolated. I hated God for letting this happen. Deep down I hated myself for failing at the one thing I could not allow myself to fail in...marriage.

The loneliness was a wolf at my door, like a dark abyss, waiting to consume me. I cried almost every night, and most mornings. I was never a drinker so there was no refuge in the bottle. I had never used drugs so that was not an option. I didn't want to date, and when I finally did try, most women could tell within the first hour that I was still in love with my ex-wife and they dropped me instantly. I missed my daughter so much it physically hurt. I was only alive when she came to my house…once a week and every other weekend. The time between her visits was like holding my breath. I was performing just enough at work to get by and pay the bills. I begged God in every way I knew to restore my marriage. He never did and then I just hated Him even more for that. I remember one morning, I was on my hands and knees weeping in pain and hurt and brokenness, and I was so mad at God that I started to scream at Him. It wasn't pretty; I was shouting the vilest obscenities at Him. Then, when I had nothing left in me, I buried my face in the carpet for a minute and sobbed. My fingers gripped the carpet so hard that I could feel the matting underneath the fibers. I ran out of tears and I was gasping in exhaustion from my sorrow. At once, I looked up and a silent scream started in my soul…my mouth was open but nothing came out. It was like the scene in Godfather Part 3 when Mary Corleone is killed and Al Pacino's character Michael drops to his knees in silence. Suddenly from his mouth comes the sound of a man's heart truly breaking. My scream burst from me like a wail. Pacino was acting; my shriek was real, as was my immense pain. I was hurtling through the vacuum of space. It was like being a captive on a roller coaster with no one at the controls.

Sometimes I would take a long look inside and the

things I saw were so terrible, and so awful, I hated myself even more. *Someone* had to be at fault in this and I was more than willing to take all the blame. I was a shipwreck and a disaster. Nobody knew what to do to help me. If they did, they never let on. People would say *"I'm praying for you"* but only one friend ever actually stopped by my pew after church, put his arm around me and said, *"I want to pray for you right now."*

It felt like all the color was draining out of my world…and my life was slowly going with it. I was suffocating in sorrow…I was worse than dead…I wasn't alive anymore. How did I get here? How did it come to this? When would my time be up in this miserable place and when could I go home? Did I still have a home?

After a few years passed, I became more functional. Not healed, just functional. I was talking to a friend once and made a remark that divorce is like "The Vietnam of Love." I felt this way because it's an ugly war that nobody approves of; the warriors who fought it don't want to talk about it because of the stigma and shame, and the public, having no experience of their own, makes rash judgments about what went on in battles they never can understand or comprehend. It is the war we don't talk about, with no heroes, no winner, and no honor for those who fought it. The more I thought about it, the more that phrase fit perfectly…"The Vietnam of Love". And here I was…a veteran. I know three men who fought in Nam. Their stories are eerily similar. I would think of those stories from time to time. I started thinking about their experiences and what I knew of battle from books I read and it was amazing how much like warfare, particularly Vietnam, divorce really is. In fact, that emotional similarity is one of the reasons I wrote this book.

When I was going through my divorce, I searched for any resource for survival written for men from a Christian perspective, but I found none.

Conversely, all I could find from a secular standpoint were books about beating my wife in court, and dating again. "Men's Health" magazine regularly runs articles about "Losing the gut and Getting back in the Game" geared at helping men re-enter the dating world. Or tax advice for divorcing dads. If I wanted to know how to come out of this like it never happened...*or like I wanted this divorce in the first place...* I could have papered City Hall with the articles. However, nobody wrote stories about the missing pictures on your walls...or in your heart. Nobody prepares you for that first time you have to tuck your daughter in by telephone, and it leaves you gasping for air between sobs. There aren't any books written about crying yourself into exhaustion until you pass out on the floor because you miss your wife, and your child and the life you were only beginning to create together. Those words had not been printed when I endured my divorce and so I had to catalog them myself. I did it because I am a great communicator in a world where men aren't always great communicators.

At any given time on any weekend in this country, there are probably hundreds, if not thousands of women's seminars going on, and many of them are based on women in divorce situations. It is practically a cottage industry. That's good, I am all for it. However, because of our societies view on masculinity, and because of how we men are wired, there isn't much out there for us. It's mostly preventive stuff, written from the assumptions that our wives are pretty submitted to us, and while they get mad, they wouldn't ever leave us because *"God hates divorce."* Well that is true God does hate divorce. Nevertheless, God's hating it doesn't seem to deter it much these days. In biblical times, a woman could not initiate a divorce, now they can go get a divorce just because they want one and we can't stop them. The world tells them it's the best thing.

Any one of the dozens of women's magazines out there will claim relationships are disposable, he isn't worth it, and the kids will adapt. It's a changed world. Therefore, I searched for a resource to help me get through it. No one from the Christian world had written any sort of a narrative about divorce.

Even a group as effective as Promise Keepers had never ventured into this arena, preferring to remain dedicated to prevention. The secular books I'd found were the "How to get Divorced Without losing everything you Owned" books, written strictly from the surgically precise standpoint of how not to lose in court. These are plentiful and written from the assumption that the man wanted the divorce, and he feels nothing at all about anything. Those books are essentially useless.

In this society, women talk about things they carry inside. But not men. Deep down inside, men are different. We don't do the "talking thing." We don't go out to O'Charley's, drink margheritas, and cry to each other. We don't bond at a weepy movie, then go for fondue, and stay up until 5 am discussing our emotions. If we even admit there is a problem, we will, at most, buy each other a beer, crack a joke involving bodily gases where someone will inevitably say "pull my finger," punch each other in the arm, and eventually just turn on the game and forget why it was we got together in the first place.

If we are really good friends with the guy who is hurting, we will go see a Schwarzenegger movie or, in case of emergency, break out the VHS of "Jaws" and repeat it line by line, trying to figure out who does the best Captain Quint impersonations and singing *"Show me the way to go home."* Any real discussion of feelings never happens, and we carry this stuff around inside us as if we swallowed a cactus. We dance around it and hint at it. But we never *talk* about it until it's in hushed tones as we see another friend flame out trying to deal with it alone. I went through this for 7 years, and I determined that if God would heal me and help me, I would let Him use me to communicate with the thousands and thousands of men who are veterans of this awful war. Or MIA in life because they are still out there on the battlefield, unable to find their way home, wandering lost and blind with gaping wounds in their hearts and in their souls. Or maybe they just got their divorce papers and they are on the verge of entering this terrible war zone, and they don't know what to do next and they wonder if this can be avoided. Every man with the divorcee's version of the "thousand yard stare", who tucks his children in by telephone, and cries more nights than he will care to admit because of the immense pain that he isn't allowed to show…that man is my brother. The guys who, this very evening will, as I did for years, work late at the office and not go home until bedtime because of the immense emptiness of their house without their family. They will walk in the door exhausted, collapse on the couch (as I did for the first 2 years because I could seldom handle sleeping in our bed by myself) and hope for sleep to give them a small refuge for a few hours. Dad's whose desks are plastered with pictures, whose refrigerators are covered with artwork, and whose planner is opened to a circled date. A date when they will next see their children and feel normal, if only for a few hours.

Maybe another reason for writing is to stop some of this from happening anymore. I would love to think that a heart or two could be changed by hearing the story of the pain I've endured. We have grown too comfortable with divorce in this country and our children, our families and our nation is paying a dear price for it. I don't want another man to hurt as I have, Or feel alone as I did, or suffer a chasm in his relationship with God because he thought God was doing this to him.

It isn't only the women who suffer in divorce. The

image of a man getting divorced and later that

week being out on the town with "two twenties" is a lie. I was a walking zombie for 8 years. I look at pictures of myself and I have aged more in the years since my divorce than any period preceding. It took years to regain any semblance of myself. When I finally got to where I wanted to make a real effort at healing, I found no resources for men, none at all. We are the true Lost Boys.

Chapter 2

A day in the life...

So, what *does* it feel like, from a man's perspective? How does a man handle losing the things for which he lives his life? What does a typical day feel like for a typical divorced man? How is my life, and my day, different from that of a married father? Myths abound and the broad brush has been liberally applied. I could write an entire book about those myths and misconceptions, but for our purposes, let's just take a snapshot view of them here. Here are the common myths about men in divorce.

Myth 1: *We all wanted the divorce.*

I wish I had time to conduct my own survey, or at least could find statistics on this subject. I know many divorced men, and more than half didn't want it. Statistics are that the woman now files 60% of divorces. I'll speak for myself here and say clearly that I didn't want mine. Things were difficult, that's for certain. Nevertheless, it could have been overcome and we could have survived and had a wonderful story of grace and hope. Now we are just a statistic. The numbers tell us that every 13 seconds a divorce is finalized in the U.S. I have to believe that the number of men involved who wanted the divorce is 50% or less. We don't all want the divorce.

Myth 2: We all cheated, abused, wouldn't work, drank, gambled...

I suppose there was a time when these things were true. Years ago, "no fault" divorces didn't exist. The only way to get a divorce was to accuse the other party of something egregious. I guess that's where these stereotypes got started and they took root in our culture. Nowadays two parties can divorce just because they want to. Nobody has to prove anything to anyone about cause. Still, the images abound of a mid-forties guy, chasing his secretary around the office while his longsuffering wife is home with the kids, suspecting, but never able to prove it. I know it happens, but not with the frequency we all think. Certainly not in the way "Lifetime" has lead us to believe. I never once even considered infidelity. That wasn't the solution to our problem and I was committed to solving it.

We had some terrible arguments and the verbal sparring escalated to extreme heights. I only learned too late that some women process verbal spats the same way they would physical abuse. Even so, arguing...even at extreme levels, isn't reason enough for divorce. It's plenty reason enough for counseling and help. I always worked sometimes multiple jobs. I don't drink. I have never been much on gambling, preferring to watch race horses and not weigh them down with my $2 ticket. As for mid-life crisis...not a chance. Marriage and family defined me. The crisis was losing that, not losing some imaginary freedoms that held no eternal value. No, most men aren't cads and bounders...we're guilty of not being perfect.

Myth 3: We are all happier now without the battles with our wives.

Do I miss the warfare? Of course. However, I missed the marriage so much more than I dreaded the fighting.

Remember; *as long as you are married, there is hope.* Hope that this can work out and you can have a successful marriage. As soon as you divorce, it's over. There is little if any chance for reconciliation then. I was not happier. Not ever. Maybe I am an optimist, but I never saw our fighting and arguments as permanent. I knew we were young and struggling and under stress. I always believed we could grow past this. Divorce takes that off the board. I don't miss arguing, but I am not *happier,* now that I am divorced.

Myth *4: We have lots of wonderful free time.*

My initial response is "yeah…so?" Free to do what? With whom? Maybe get in a round of golf every other Saturday morning without having to ask my wife? Maybe go out to a club or a ballgame without checking in or making arrangements? There's no comfort there for me. I suppose there are selfish guys who look at it like that. *"Now I am free and I can come and go as I please"* Those aren't the guys I'm talking about here, and they probably aren't the kind of men who will ever read this book. In fact, they are the guys for whom the broad-brush was created.

However, most divorced men I've met have the same opinion…this isn't fun. It isn't a chance to re-live my carefree college days. I miss my daughter too much on days when I am doing something fun. I miss being married. Long after I got over my wife and stopped loving her and missing her…I still missed being married. That's how I'm built, and I have been surprised to find out how many other men are built the same way. My free time is not free…it came with a huge price tag attached. I pay for it with all the tears I've cried, and still cry. I pay for it with all the lonely nights and dinners for one and memories, I am missing with my daughter.

Myth 5: *We date 20-somethings and re-live our college days.*

Not even close. Maybe there are guys out there who do. In fact, I know of a couple. However, they are strange guys anyway, divorced or not. What do I have in common with a 20 year old, besides her parents taste in music? Why would I want to be with someone whom I have absolutely nothing in common with? I have a daughter, when she is in her twenties; would I be okay with her bringing a man my age home with her? Are you kidding? I don't just live for me, I am a dad. Aside from the psychological, emotional, spiritual, and physical differences, I am a dad. I have an example to set, and I wouldn't want someone around my daughter who is closer to her age than mine. The whole "proving myself sexually" thing is lost on me. Being with a 20-year-old college coed wouldn't make me a man in any way at all. We'll discuss sexual purity after divorce in another chapter, but my snapshot here is this…the same rules apply before you married for the first time. The marriage bed is undefiled, anything else is sin.

Myth 6: *It's all behind me now and I seldom think about it.*

Ha! I wish! I wish I didn't think about it. I wish there weren't a thousand daily reminders of my social status. It happens when I fill out a form or file my taxes. It happens when I show up for one of Morgan's school activities and I am the single dad. It happens when I am invited out to lunch after church, or when I am sitting there in worship, surrounded by families. I haven't had five minutes in all the years since my divorce, where I wasn't reminded of it. There could be another dozen myths on this list, but I'll stop here. The point is, they abound. Everyone thinks they know what happened and everyone thinks they have some solution. The truth is nobody remotely understands the devastation a divorce renders in the lives of the parties involved…and the men hurt just as much.

I have been divorced 13 years as of this writing and I only within the last three years even considered dating seriously. I don't have the heart and I am afraid. Period. I am afraid I will fail again, even though I know in my heart that my divorce was only half my fault. Even though it was my ex wife who initiated the divorce and she had no biblical grounds. None of that matters. I am still petrified. I couldn't bear a second failure at the very thing I couldn't bear failing at *once*. For years, it felt like there is no room in my heart for the kind of pain I have already endured so I suppose there isn't room in my heart for anyone at all except my daughter. It's a risk I couldn't bring myself to take. The manageable pain of loneliness was superior to the unknown pain of failure.

Beyond that, I don't ever miss an opportunity to see my daughter. I haven't abandoned her nor am I a deadbeat, quite the opposite. I look for opportunities to spend even an extra 30 minutes with her. I will go have lunch with her or pick her up after school just to drive her home and spend 10 minutes in the car with her, just talking. I miss her every single moment of the day. I am not a "bachelor" all over again. I don't enjoy having guaranteed free weekends, and nobody home at night. I am not a party animal who is relishing his second chance at his college lifestyle. I get lonely. I miss what was supposed to have been happening by this stage of my life. I miss my daughter when she is not here. I miss being married. I don't necessarily miss my wife. She is remarried and has had another child and I wish her well. However, I loved being married and we should have stuck it out because that is what people are supposed to do.

I liked having someone to live for and dream for and set goals for and I miss that and for a long time it embittered me. I hurt daily because my daughter is growing up under these circumstances and she is learning the pain that I promised her she never would feel, before she was even born. I never, ever wanted to be a divorcee and I certainly never wanted this for my precious child. I wanted better.

Make no mistake, staying together is *better*. Period. I know there are exceptions and I am not attacking anyone's particular situation. I have dear friends who divorced to save their lives...literally. I am not referring to you. I am referring to frivolous, "I want something else" divorces. Divorces because someone didn't get rich enough fast enough. Divorces because someone put on 30 pounds or went grey prematurely. Divorces driven by self and self alone. I don't know what the percentages are and I'm not here to discuss that. I'm here to decry the ease with which we dismiss marriage and family and the pain it brings. It hurts me. I am very disappointed with the way things turned out and it shows itself in many ways. My job drags. My enthusiasm wanes from time to time.

However, every time I talk to a divorced man I hear the same frustrations and the same disappointments. I know there are some guys who initiated it, who wanted out, and who were abusive jerks. But that's not all of us; in fact, it's not most of us. It's just that those guys get the press and we are sucked along in the wake. Most of us endure to the end, love our kids, and stick it out. Many of us never remarry because we never get over the fear or the hurt of that initial failure. On the outside, it looks like we are selfish or disinterested, but the truth is we are afraid. What if we allow ourselves to fall in love again, make another commitment, allow someone new into our child's life and then *that fails too*? How could we rebound from that a second time? How could our children? In addition to that, we are so busy waging constant battles with the whole divorce system that we never have time to find love anyway. The entire court system is geared toward the mother now. That's not a bitter dad speaking...it's a fact. I researched some things online once and was surprised to find a term called *"Disenfranchised Fathers Syndrome"* I was amazed.

Lest you think it was invented by some woman-hating man, it was not. It was developed by a female psychologist. She maintains that there are few, if any, real deadbeat dads. Most of those we call deadbeat dads are really disenfranchised. The divorce court system has so beaten them up and worked so hard to remove them from their children's lives that they just give up. They feel useless and worthless in the lives of their families so they become just that. The system is no longer equitable and they know it. They spend their lives trying to remain a dad...trying to hold on to that precious fatherhood that they never asked to be abridged.

I know...I see men fight this battle all the time. We are sent the clear message from the court that we don't matter except where monthly child support is concerned. We have little input. We have little say in the daily life of our children unless we force the matter. When we do, we are dragged back into court or at least threatened with such action. "If you want my rights you will have to fight for them" is the message that is sent, and that costs lots of money. There is a subtle underlying fear at work here too. Who would want to involve herself with a man with this much of an anchor weighing him down? What woman would want to align herself with a guy who is in court a couple of times each year because of an ongoing battle with an ex-wife who won't relent and simply let him be a dad?

It's unattractive. Moreover, the choice eventually becomes, leave behind my devotion to my daughter, or leave behind the opportunity for a relationship. I will never forsake the former to pursue the latter. So my choice is already made. We never stop thinking about our kids. I can't stop being a dad or put it in park when my daughter isn't with me. I worry, I pray, I call to check on her. I schedule parent conferences with teachers. I try to do all the things I would have done while I was married to her mom. It helps me to feel like a dad, but it's a poor substitute.

I miss her minute by minute. I grieve the loss of time with her. It's selfish I know, because I know there are people who have lost a child forever and it's not the same as what I feel. My own family faced such a loss. But it still hurts to miss her so much. I have never gotten used to an empty bedroom or not hearing her prayers every evening. I am a part time daddy with a full time daddy's heart. The two don't coexist easily. I miss the image I held of holidays and birthdays and vacations and events. Those things won't ever look or feel the way they were supposed to and they hurt me even thirteen years later…and I suppose they will forever to some degree.

There is sadness to my life that I will readily admit to. I can't help it. This isn't a situation that will rectify itself. I am happy, but I am sad too. I am fulfilled, but I remain empty in some areas. I am a dad without the object of his fatherly affections always present. I am a man who loved deeply and planned on living out that love for the rest of my life with the same person. I am a man who notices the absences on alternating Christmas mornings and the awkwardness of being alone at family gatherings. I once, long ago, painted a picture of how I hoped my life would be. My picture had a wife, children, and a home. I do a thousand things alone that I had always hoped to do as a family. Church, vacations, evening walks, weddings, parties, cookouts. You name it. Most people progress towards a vision for their life that they have developed over the years. Mine...and I dare say most men...included the one person I would love forever, and the children that love would produce. We would have our hardships and difficulties to be sure, but that is what makes the enduring journey worth it.

The toll along the road to a lifetime together is paid in blood sweat and tears. It isn't all happiness and romance, but it is a slow building of a life and the dreams you share. One day, you wake up and can't imagine a life separate from this person...warts and all. I don't think we are built in a way that allows that to all be destroyed and then recreated with someone else. Maybe I'm wrong...I hope I am...but I see so many people enter into second marriages with cynicism and skepticism. It failed once when I wasn't expecting it to. I'll never be caught off guard again. Love is redefined as something less than the mystical, wonderful, fanciful, romantic hurricane that sweeps you along in its fury. Now it is measured, calculated, careful, and constrained. There are exceptions I know, people who are "serial marriers" but most of us are not. Most of us have lost the magic and now only hope for the leftovers or don't even bother believing in it anymore. My mental pictures were crystal clear. Divorce took those I love most from that picture, but their silhouette remains and it just serves to make their absence more noticeable. Divorce has left its mark, and its mark is a hole that doesn't fill.

That is what it feels like to be me for a day.

Chapter 3

A Brief History of the World

How did I ever end up divorced?

Maybe the only thing more unlikely than me being divorced is me writing a book about it. I guess it's like any other hostile situation…it doesn't start out with hostility. In fact, for me, it started out as a dream come true. But before all that, some history might be in order. Here's some basic information.

I was born on Sept. 7 1963, in Chester PA, just a stones throw from Philadelphia. The home I grew up in was actually in Philly. If you've ever flown into Philadelphia International Airport on a Jumbo Jet, you took off or landed on the longest runway, which runs parallel to the Delaware River. This also means you flew right over my grandmothers' house on 4th Avenue. This was my home for the first 4 ½ years of my life.

My mother and father never married and so my mother and I lived with my grandparents because my mother worked. My grandfather was the son of Ukraine immigrants and was a WWII veteran. He served with the Seabees in the Pacific theatre. He was a troubled man who drank as if he was being paid by the glass. I have about a half dozen memories of "Big Jake" sober; he lived out all but his final days under the influence. My mother was 20 when I was born and my father was 22. My father is also the son of immigrants. My paternal grandparents emigrated here from Italy around 1895. My grandfather hails from Montecassino, which, during the Renaissance was a cultural center without rival.

My father was the second youngest of 15 children. I've only ever spoken to him face to face on one occasion. He had a burning desire to finish college, and be the first from his large, very poor family to attain a college degree. My father had a lifelong love of learning, culminating in a PhD in education he achieved in his fifties. He passed this love to my daughter and me. The years in between my birth and my marriage are not without great import, but as this is not a biography, I will resist going there in this writing. But it is important to know some background because each divorce throws open a door inside the heart of the divorcee and makes you look at the things that got you here. Because the truth is that all divorces have their sinister root in something or some things from long ago. You have to know yourself, and know yourself well. Deep secrets of the heart will do much to contribute to the destruction of a marriage. They will also determine how well you handle the divorce.

We all have baggage but not all of us can recognize all of it. I know I didn't. I had been to counseling, I had read books, and I had gone to men's group meetings. However, there are things lurking in the closets of every human heart, and sometimes someone else has the key to that door. Sometimes only interaction with someone else can bring those issues to the fore. That is why so many people seem "different" when they are in a relationship. Because they are being forced to face some things that only interaction can bring out. In extreme cases, this is a personality disorder. There are men and women who are great folks until you have to live with them or work with them. Casually, they are gregarious and charming, but personally and relationally, they are dysfunctional. Much of that springs from the well that was dug early in their lives. If left unattended, it becomes a root of bitterness and a destroyer of relationships. You simply have to look backwards sometimes if you want to move forward successfully. Sometimes that is painful and sometimes it hurts more than just you in the process. Nevertheless, if you leave the past swept under your rug it grows teeth and gains power in your life and it will *always* resurface. Therefore, while there are aspects of this writing that are personal to me and uncomfortable for some readers, they are necessary. They are here as an example of where to look and what doors to kick in as you try to heal the wounds that might sabotage *your* marriage someday…or have already.

"When love comes to town"

God had specifically brought Holly and me together…or so it seemed. There was a moment when we both felt it was His doing, and from that moment on, we planned on getting married. We met on Valentines Day 1996, and she was the most beautiful woman I'd ever seen. We dated long distance for a year and married on Valentines Day 1997. It wasn't long after that the first shots were fired, but at first, it was wonderful. I loved being married. I loved everything about it. I was 32 and had been single for all of my adult life and I was ready for marriage. I loved defining myself as a husband. I loved dreaming dreams for us and listening to Holly's dreams and thinking of ways to try to make them come true. The only problem was, I was so poorly equipped to do that. I didn't have the ability to fulfill her dreams, heal her wounds, or patch the huge holes in her heart, this lead to disappointment for both of us. She was disappointed in me because I couldn't meet these needs, and I was disappointed in my disappointing her. Conversely, I needed to be defined as a man by being a success as a husband and I was not doing a very good job at it. This ate away at my own value as a man and started me on a downward spiral of trying to be everything and do everything right so I could finally be defined as a "grown up" man. The tension mounted quickly and the first fight happened at the 3-month mark. It seemed like suddenly we were at war. I got married February 14 1997. It was Valentines Day, a Friday, and the one year anniversary of the day Holly and I met for the first time. We were both nervous and wondering what we were in for. Holly had moved to my home in Delaware from Utah where she grew up. We didn't want to live together outside of marriage, and she didn't want to move in with strangers. We knew we wanted to be married so we had a small ceremony at our church and planned a big wedding in Utah that fall. I don't know what started our first fight…nerves, disappointment, fear. But we started fighting almost right away. Not anything serious at first, but just stupid things. Nevertheless, they were a precursor of what was around the corner, only we didn't know it at the time. Looking back, I think they were just the stupid, petty irritations that people experience as they become more adjusted to living together as a married couple. At first, Holly had very unrealistic, somewhat immature expectations of marriage. Rather than address them realistically and honestly, I chose the path of least resistance and tried to live up to them. They were nonsensical really. The stupid, inane things like leaving the seat up, listening to different kinds of music than each other cares for, and not liking the others' favorite restaurant. It was little, nothing arguments that, under normal circumstances amount to a good laugh when you look back on them. However, the truth was that Holly and I both came from such damaged backgrounds that every argument seemed enormous. Neither of us came from a very good homelife and I think we were both so afraid that we'd end up like our parents that we ended up like our parents. We were both hurting inside and needed more from a marriage than a marriage was intended to deliver. Marriages tend to exaggerate everything in one's life…the good and the bad. If you are strong and healthy, they make you stronger and healthier. However, if you are hurting and needy inside with holes that need filling, marriage can make you hurt more, need more, and make your holes even bigger.

I think the first real knockdown, drag out fight we had occurred about three months after we were married and it was about money. Most of our fights were about finances. In hindsight, that was an area where we needed to get counseling and guidance before we ever got together. My parents were terrible with money and hers were too. I never took any steps to correct that deficit in my family tree and it came home to roost very early. But in reality…it could have been anything. Because looking back on it, and looking back through my family history, the vicious fights were inevitable…all it took was a catalyst. I remember driving home one evening and listening to Focus on the Family. The guest was some counselor who had written a book about relationships and he was discussing five signs that your relationship was in deep trouble. I don't remember what the first four were, but I remember the last one. He said "If one or both spouses instantly "go for the throat" in an argument, virtually without provocation, saying the absolute worst things possible to inflict the most damage right away…you have a problem" This sent a chill down my spine. Holly had been, for about 2 months by this point, going for the kill in every little petty argument. She would instantly make a hurtful remark about my parents, my father's rejection of me, and my failures financially, or anything else she could say to draw blood immediately. My initial response was to be defensive, and that prevented me from seeing what the real issues were. I never stepped back from her hurtful words to see why she was doing this. She was angry, she was sad, she was scared. Because our marriage wasn't what she had hoped for immediately, she felt betrayed and deceived. She had an image built up in her mind of how I was supposed to be and it was a standard I could not live up to. Instead of addressing that, I eventually started fighting back. That's the insidious nature of this war…like all wars I suppose…you get to the point where you can't tell who the enemy is. In Vietnam, the enemy used to booby-trap babies and hide behind women and children. In the divorce war, Satan, (the real enemy) disguises himself in the actions of the one you love; he ambushes you from his hiding place that he cleverly disguises as the anger in your wife's voice and the fire in her eyes. He finds a foothold and conceals himself within the hurtful words you both speak to each other and before you know it; your hearts are caught in your own crossfire. You are really fighting Satan and his evil schemes from hell itself, aimed at destroying you, your marriage, your family, and your dreams. He is so clever at disguising himself, that you think your enemy is the person you swore you'd love honor and cherish. I can't remember how long we had been married when Holly first threatened divorce. It was probably around the 6-month mark. Money was once again the issue and she dropped the charge… "If this doesn't get better, I'm leaving you." And that was it, the war had begun. I had been served notice. The clock was ticking and I had a performance to deliver or I was going to be shipped out. Unfortunately, under that kind of pressure, no one can really deliver. It was the bottom of the ninth, full count and I had not gotten a hit yet. If I didn't hit a home run right now, the game was over and my side would lose. Well, I struck out repeatedly, and each time the warnings grew louder. She would fire a shot, and at first, I tried to send out a peace envoy. I would bring her flowers or take her for a ride and tell her how things would be better. I told her I had a plan but deep inside I had none. All I knew was my wife, who I adored, was going to leave me and I was scared witless. I began to operate totally out of fear. I began to make desperate decisions in an attempt to keep from losing my wife. To add to the pressure, we had been married seven months when we found out we were pregnant. I was at once excited and frightened. I always wanted to be a daddy, but we were broke and struggling and the fights had already grown in severity and duration. Now a baby was coming.

Holly was from Utah and I was born in Philadelphia and grew up nearby in Wilmington DE. She hated the Philadelphia area. We were gruff, abrupt Yankees who shot from the hip and gave no quarter...and that was to the people we loved. So, in an effort to keep her happy and maybe secure a peace and avoid the looming battle, I moved my 4-month pregnant wife to Nashville, where we both had mutual friends and we thought she'd be happier. I didn't particularly want to leave my home, but I thought that if she was happy I could be happy anywhere. I was wrong. In retrospect, leaving the only support group we had, whether Holly saw them that way at the time or not, pretty much sealed our fate. Nevertheless, my wife was miserable, I loved her, and so I took her side against my roots and my hometown and moved. This was a mistake on many fronts. Not because Nashville is a bad town, but because we knew almost no one. The few people we knew were not friends on the level that they would get involved in our situation and help us survive. So we were further isolated and Holly was just as unhappy as we were in Delaware. We were just as broke, and we fought even more. I was truly scared.

Sadly, Nashville didn't fix anything...we were fighting every day by this point. It always started with money but it would quickly escalate into anything and everything. Like a wildfire, it just burned up anything around it that could be used for fuel. We had a baby coming and we were living in an apartment, we had no nursery. Holly and I knew almost nobody and so she never had a real baby shower. Every day she was telling me she was leaving me and it made me resent her. I resented her because I was scared and because I felt like all my efforts were being ignored. I felt like she was finding it so easy to tell me she would throw our marriage away. It made me think I valued her more than she valued me. It made me feel like I was the only one in love in this marriage. We would go to church and seek prayer but nothing changed. I was going through the motions spiritually. I couldn't admit that I didn't have the answers...that would look weak, or so I thought, and I didn't think she could handle me looking weak. She had asked me a few times to go for pastoral counseling but I refused. I was going to fix this myself, show her how smart I was, and prove myself to her, and to God, (who by now I felt I was also failing). Besides...I didn't want my pastor to know how I was failing as a man and a husband. My pastor at the time had been a true friend from the moment we arrived in

Nashville and started attending that church. He would have helped me and not chided me, but my pride wouldn't let me seek his help. I couldn't let him know what was happening. I didn't want any man to know. That is the insidious nature of being a man these days. The very thing I needed to do was to open up, expose my weaknesses, and gain the strength and wisdom from others. But that was too big a threat to me because it would require me to drop my guard and admit I wasn't strong enough and didn't have all the answers. This flies in the face of modern manhood. In the end, mired in my weakness and isolated by my own manhood, I couldn't fix it, and the battle grew worse. I was scared and wounded. I could see what was coming and my fear only made me angrier. I felt so disposable to Holly. That scared me even more, and the battles raged and the air grew colder in our home. I was becoming someone I never thought I could be. I felt like an observer of my own life. I was…*we* were…hurtling toward devastation and destruction and I think we both knew it. We were afraid and that made it worse. Subconsciously, I believe we had both reached a point where it was "my way or the highway" and neither was willing to give any ground to the other. More than anything, I was losing myself in my fear and misery and losing my wife in the process.

Chapter 4

This Isn't Really Me

I don't remember the date…

…I probably should; looking back it was a very important date indeed. But I never thought about writing it down. Actually, there were two dates; two individual events that changed me at my core and pushed us past the point of no return. The first one happened about 6 months after we were married. Holly and I had been arguing a lot and the fights escalated in intensity almost weekly. She had begun going right for my heart in every argument by now, saying whatever it took to cut me the deepest and inflict the most pain. One time it was a comment about my father and his rejection of me being very understandable, as if he knew something about me that no one else did. Another time it would be an attack on my adopted family that cut me to my soul. I believe it was a comment about her sudden attraction to a handsome doctor she worked with that started the fight in question. She came home from work and we drifted into another argument about money. Before I knew it, she was confessing her attraction to this doctor and hinting that "if she were single" he would make a great catch. After all, he was wealthy. In my heart, I wanted to believe that she would never do something like that, and she was trying to hurt me to make her point, (which was wrong of her by the way. I'm not excusing either party here) but I didn't do much thinking. This was too much and we really started screaming at each other. We were lying on the bed and I said something that hurt her and she started punching at me. She had done this before and I was never really bothered by it. I am 6'4" and she is 5'7"…it wasn't as if she did any physical damage. However, this time she was straddling me as I lay there on the bed and she really hit me pretty hard. It made me mad and I knew that I needed to get away from her hitting me before it escalated. I rolled to my right to try to get off the bed and as I did it, I instinctively swung my hand at her to get her away from me. And in the course of doing this I hit my wife.

I didn't cock my arm back and ball my fist and punch, in fact it was a reaction to her punching me and I was merely trying to get away from her…but still, I slapped at her in anger during a confrontation, and I felt my soul leave me. In a moment of stress…being struck by a woman for the first time in my adult life, I modeled the very response I detested. In hindsight, it wasn't that I really hit her; it was that I was angry enough that I even came close. I *never ever* saw myself in that position. This wasn't *me*. I was carrying around so much self-loathing and so much fear of losing her and fear of failure, that I wasn't thinking clearly anymore. I was on edge from the stress and fear of watching my marriage disintegrating. She was reminding me of what I already thought about myself… that she deserved better than I could provide…I didn't deserve her, etc. It became too much and I lost control. Something in my soul died that day. I think it was my innocence. My home was turning into the home in which I had grown up. My marriage was beginning to model that of my parents. My heart was dying in my chest and I lost a part of my soul. While I never raised my hand to my wife again after that day, the verbal wars escalated at an exponential rate. I didn't really have to raise my hand to her. The wall would do…or the doorjamb. Anything I could swing at instead of her that would send the message, *"I'm hurt and angry, and you can't leave because I'm big and I say so."* I hate that behavior, I had grown up with that, and it made my skin crawl. However, I had not taken the steps before my marriage to remove those roots and so I just fell into the pattern my parents had modeled for me. It made me sick, but by the time I realized what was happening, I think things were too far-gone. By now, something had died…some boundary was crossed, some spiritual wall had crumbled, and I was no longer innocent.

What I really was, was scared. I was losing everything that mattered to me and I knew it and I did everything I shouldn't have. It was slipping away and I was powerless so I tried to appear powerful. Nothing could have been more wrong for the situation. After that, the words were far more cutting, delivered with a much louder, more intimidating boom and the desired effect now was not reason and solution, but bullying and fear. To be fair to myself, in hindsight, I showed tremendous restraint. My ex-wife had a terrible problem with violence and would hit me regularly. Being a very big man and having an old fashioned viewpoint, I never could respond in kind, but the blows were humiliating and emasculating and pushing that sort of emotion down inside only makes it surface somewhere else as something else. For us it was the verbal warfare.

Maybe something in my heart gave in that day and I just figured nothing would work except intimidation. My army was bigger and stronger so she had better do what I wanted. I know one thing...I had become, in that one instant, everything I detested and swore I never would be. Something many vets echo. As little boys, we grow up playing "army" in our back yards, killing imaginary bad guys who represent real evil. We don't know what they look like but we are sure they are ugly, twisted, and bad and they deserved to die. The world is better when we rid it of this pretend enemy. The problem is when the battlefront is in your own home the enemy doesn't look like you imagined it would, and instead of feeling like a hero, you just feel sick. The tragic nature of marital battles is that the enemy of your soul has disguised himself as the very person you love the most...and you don't even know why you are at war.

That was the first real event of our marriage. The second event happened about two months later. We were living in Nashville by this point and the arguments had grown in frequency and intensity. One night she came home and told me about the resident doctors at the hospital she worked at who were hitting on her. They were flirting with my wife and telling her how they were going to be wealthy and they would take care of her in ways that I couldn't. Then she said, *"the next time I marry it will be for money and not love. I'm tired of being poor. You can't take care of me so maybe I should find someone who can*" In an instant, I got her in my sights, clicked off the safety and took my best shot...wanting to hurt her as much as I could, but without a physical attack, of course, I decided to hit her emotionally. I opened my mouth and hit her with just one word. I said something I regret to this day, in fact, I regretted it as soon as I said it but the damage was done. Holly looked at me with a look of such hurt and betrayal and I've never forgotten that look. Now, she shouldn't have said what she said, and she hurt me, but I chose to respond in kind and I did tremendous damage that day. Whatever was left of my innocence and of the wonder and magic we felt for each other was gone after that. We fought all the time now, and for any reason. I hated what was becoming of us. I was crazy about my wife and I was so hurt, afraid, and insecure. It sickened me to see what this war was doing to us. The saddest part was that the one Source of healing for us was, being totally left out of our life together. My job as the spiritual leader of my family was to lead us to Him and seek the answers, but I was too proud to do that, and she was too far from Him to be led back. To seek God by this point would require my admitting my part of the failure and I had retreated into self-defense mode and was no longer interested in a peaceful resolution. I also made the basic mistake that many spouses make...I felt like me running to God for help would be useless if I did it alone. I felt like if Holly didn't agree to pursue the spiritual help we needed along with me, what was the point of me doing it by myself? In retrospect, that was critically foolish. I should have run to God simply because it was the thing to do with or without her. I should have fallen on His grace and mercy, prayed diligently, and hoped for Him to change us both. Instead, I grew more spiritually isolated. Somewhere inside I blamed God for all of this, and she did too. Why didn't He step in and fix our problems? Where was He? My pastor back in Delaware, my dear spiritual daddy Paul Walters, once told me that the Holy Spirit is *"the perfect Gentleman…He only goes where he is invited and He never overstays His welcome"* I've told that to dozens of people over the years but when I needed to heed that advice I never did. God wasn't going to force His way into our situation, and I was too proud and too embarrassed by my failings to invite Him. He was eagerly waiting by the door hoping against hope for us to invite Him into our mess. But we never did…I never did. Once again, my pride was in the way and I was determined to show everyone…including God, that I could do this. I could be a husband and a dad and I could save us from this awful nightmarish battle. I would prove my worth to my wife and to the world, and to God in the process, by solving all our problems, making it big, winning father of the year, healing our wounds, and making good on every promise I'd made.

Who was I kidding? I was alone in the world, separated from my friends and family and rejecting the warnings of my God. It's a wonder I made it out at all. You'd think I'd have had some "fox-hole religion" but the opposite was true. I took all my misery, wounded pride, broken dreams, and empty promises, wrapped them in the remnants of my marriage, and blamed them all on God. The truth was that deep down inside I was so ashamed of what I was, of the awful things I'd done on the battlefield that my home had become, that I couldn't see God wanting to help me any more. No, I was going to figure this all out myself and then I would have nobody to thank but me. It wasn't until years later that I understood how much God was hurting for Holly, Me, and Morgan. Christ died for *these sins too.* I had lost sight of that fact and felt like I couldn't be forgiven. Looking back, I understand why Paul says to watch out for a root of bitterness springing up amongst us. Once it does, it bears some awful fruit. A bitter spirit takes up all the room in your heart and the Holy Spirit can't work. I had long ceased to listen to God's prompting and I paid the price for it.

Going it Alone...

War and battles are probably amongst the things to which men most easily relate. We're all fans of war history and we watch the TV shows about the military. I suppose that's one reason I made the parallel between military battles and military lifestyle, and the enduring battle of divorce. I think the camaraderie we see in war stories is an attraction to us as men. If you look at the way battles were fought, it's easy to understand the bond that formed.

In WW1, trench warfare was the way most battles were fought. Even today, we still use this term to define the daily shoulder-to-shoulder grind of the workplace or of life in general. A hard working, meat and potatoes blue-collar guy is said to be working "down in the trenches." The rugged offensive and defensive lineman are said to be the guys "fighting it out in the trenches." They are the often overlooked, not very glamorous, "muckers and grinders" as we hockey players like to call ourselves. They are guys who know that no matter how strong they are, their strength is always multiplied when they depend on the guys to the left and to the right. Safety in numbers is their motto and it gets them farther than they can ever get alone. The battles in WW1 were no different. Look at old photos of that war sometime. The men were fighting for their lives, shoulder to shoulder. There was strength and relative safety in numbers. It was easier to be less afraid when you saw a hundred men on either side of you. They lived and died as one man. No one kept secrets in that sort of an environment.

Jump ahead to WW2, the trench had been replaced by the foxhole. The foxhole was not nearly as large. Maybe 4 to 6 guys in a hole. Still, you weren't fighting alone. You still had other men to draw strength from, and other men drew strength from you. You shared each other's mail and each other's meals. You could rely on each other, and many a successful revision to a battle plan was hatched by a brainstorming session, under fire, in a foxhole with men you knew and trusted. These guys had been through the worst with you and you relied on them. They would die for you and you would die for them. Each man had entrusted the sending of the last letter home, to the other men in his unit if he didn't make it, and they all knew you'd do the same for them. They knew each other. They trusted each other. Running through each man's mind at the time of the most intense fighting and subsequent intense fear, was the knowledge that the other guys were counting on me and I am counting on them. This made it a little easier to give it that one final push that made the difference between winning and losing. Between beating back the attack of the enemy or surrender and capture. This is why there is so much camaraderie amongst WW2 vets even today. There is a joy in reunion with these old vets that many other vets don't share. Why? Perhaps it is because they truly fought as one man.

Now jump ahead to Vietnam, and see a far different style of warfare…and very sadly, a real archetype for the way men relate in stress situations like divorce.

Vietnam was, by nature, impossible to fight using either of the aforementioned strategies. There were no trenches and virtually no foxholes. The reasons are several. One was the jungle. The jungle was unlike almost anything we had seen in wartime before. With the exception of some of the battles of the Pacific Theater in WW2, all our fighting until that point had been in a city or countryside setting, against a clearly defined enemy wearing a uniform different from ours.

In Vietnam, we fought in the thickest, densest jungle known to man. The enemy wasn't on the other side of some line on a map, he was everywhere, and he looked like everyone. He didn't wear a uniform. He booby-trapped babies, old people, and peaceful villages. You couldn't dig in and hold a position for more than a few hours or days because he was everywhere and he was so numerous. Therefore, we fought a battle where the majority of the time our soldiers were walking patrols. They were in a fire line about ten feet apart and they were always moving. Occasionally you would hunker down for an ambush or holding point, but for the most part, you moved. You didn't stop moving at all. Busy, active, no time to seize ground and regroup.

Today it is no different. The pace of our lives makes it hard to bond with fellows warriors. This makes it hard to know the guy next to you. He isn't sitting with you in a foxhole with enemy fire bursting around your ears; he is ten feet from you. You can see him but you can't touch him or lean on him if you were weary in battle. It is isolating in a way other wars have not been. The sad thing is that this mirrors what has happened amongst men in our society. It's been happening for years and years now. We have grown colder toward each other, more afraid in our battles and less able to admit it. Just when we need each other the most, the style of warfare we are engaged in has drawn us apart. I can look to my left or my right and I can see my brother but he is just a little too far to help me and the battle is too intense right now for him to hear my cries for help. I know if he could see me, he'd return some fire and buy me some time, but he is in his own hot zone and he can't slow down to lend me a hand.

Maybe, if he can beat the enemy back just a little, he can make it over here to my position and lend me some support, but it isn't likely. He is fighting for his own life and in the rare moments when he manages to cast me a glance, if I look closely, I can see the same fear in his eyes that I show in mine. Since childhood, society has been drilling us not to show fear and not to give up our ground. I wish they had told us to band together. I wish they realized that two men could defend more ground and take back more of the enemy territory than any number of singular soldiers ever can. They've been training us this way for so long that they don't know anything else. It would require a complete restructuring of our way of training and thinking to change now, and we don't have time for that with this battle going on. Nobody seems to notice that we are losing.

I wish I knew how many times I wanted someone to talk to when the wheels were coming off my wagon. When the enemies were storming the gates of my home and the "zips were in the wire" all around and I was overrun, I had no one to call on and to cry out to for some help and some reinforcement. I saw all my friends busy in their own firefights and I figured they were too busy for me to bother them. If only we had stood our ground together, maybe more of us would have won. Proverbs teaches us "As iron sharpens iron, so one man sharpens another." These days, not much real sharpening is going on, and men are dying alone in the jungle, mere inches from each other. It breaks my heart. What difference would camaraderie have made? What words could have been spoken and what acts of kindness would have meant the most.

About 25 years ago, I read a book titled "The Friendless American Male." The premise of the book is that men make all their closest friends by about age 23. Once we graduate college and get out into the world, we don't develop deep friendships. We spend too much time acquiring a home and building a life for our family. We don't open up easily and our competitive nature prohibits us from dropping our guard enough to really develop friendships. This is doubly dangerous for a guy like me who moved from his hometown to a city where he knows virtually no one. I can say unequivocally that after 15 years in Nashville, I still have no one here that I call a real true friend in the way I do the guys I grew up with. That's nobody's fault, it's just our nature.

One hope I have for this book is that it will enlighten people on how to really truly minister to a divorced man. I have documented this journey so that these will no longer be uncharted waters. I've spoken my heart and revealed my own tears, so that no man need live through this alone ever again. We all need a friend who really understands and really knows us. Our ragged pace and closed, fearful society has made that almost impossible. We need it now more than ever and now more than ever it is so hard to find.

Chapter 5

Nobody Knows You
When You're Down and Out

I heard all sorts of comments and received all kinds of advice in the years after my divorce...

...My family handled it in varying ways. My brother, who had suffered through his own unhappy marriage and divorce, said little. He told me how sorry he was and that he understood. He spoke occasionally of the hurt he felt, but in all he didn't have much to offer in the way of comfort. In part, because at that point he was still relatively new to his own divorce pain and because he knew that there was little anyone could really do or say. He was going through his own spiritual struggles and had nothing to offer in comfort from a Christian perspective.

My stepfather, as usual, said nothing. He never called when I was going through the rocky times in my marriage, never called after we were divorced and never attempted to connect or bond in the years after. He probably to this day wouldn't even know how hurting I was back then, and my father was just not there...not ever.

In my heart, I longed for my father. I wished I could have drawn on his advice and wisdom. I needed him to tell me he had observed me as a husband, a father and I had done a decent job, and sometimes your best just isn't good enough. I needed his approval as a man and his pronouncement that I wasn't a failure, but I could get neither.

My mother handled it quite differently. Her response was mind-boggling. Her first reaction was to attack Holly. Suddenly I was bombarded with a laundry list of things she never liked about her in the first place. She tore into everything she could think of concerning my ex-wife. She suddenly didn't like the way she looked or wore make-up or her hairstyle. She conveniently confided in me how she never liked the sound of Holly's voice or her taste in clothing. She insisted Holly had treated me terribly while we were married. She had once told my wife that she'd married the wrong son and that she should have married my brother...now she was telling me she never liked her to begin with. I had grown accustomed to this behavior and ignored it. After I had been divorced about six months, her attitude began to change.

While she riled against Holly to me, she was secretly calling her at her office to arrange to talk to Morgan. Holly refused to speak to her but she would tell me about the phone calls and I would have felt betrayed if not for the fact that I was so used to her unpredictable actions that nothing could surprise me anymore. I had been divorced about 2 years and I was home for Christmas with Morgan. My mother, Morgan, and I went to my cousin's house to visit her and her family.

My cousin's husband was there along with their two daughters and my cousin's mom, my aunt Donna. I loved being with my family, especially around the holidays, but at one point it served to remind me of the wonderful perfect picture I had painted for my own family. Being with them suddenly reminded me that I was not going to have that picture ever. Even if I remarry one day, my daughter will be forced to share her holidays with two families and maybe that's not always what she'll want to do. We left the house that afternoon and my mother tore into me in the car. She proclaimed how embarrassed she was to see me so sullen. I had ruined, she claimed, everyone's Christmas celebration and they had all privately told her so. This was not actually the case as I asked my aunt Donna a few years later and she told me nobody had said a word to her. My mom just wanted to say what she felt but put the blame on someone else. In her eyes, I had grieved enough and now I was just embarrassing. It's cruel and heartless I know but I am sure that others have felt that way. Not just in my case but in many cases. People tend to care only to the point of being made to feel slightly uncomfortable, and nothing more beyond that. I remember being at a party one time and a friend of mine came over and sat down and asked me how I was doing. She said it with real concern and I felt she was genuine. I told her I was still very hurting and very sad. I missed Holly, I missed Morgan, and I missed being married. She asked me what Holly was doing and at that time, Holly had been getting a little wild on the days she didn't have Morgan. I had gotten wind of it and it broke my heart even further. When I began to speak to my friend about these things, she just stood up and walked away. Now, she was not a friend of Holly's at all so it was not because she was uncomfortable hearing it. She was a person who wanted to surround herself with "positive" people and didn't like to hear any "negative energy" talk. In other words, she was a post 60's hippie with no concept of reality.

Nobody wants to hang out with Bad Luck Shleprock, I'll admit, but it's a fallen world, and a lot of the energy out there is negative. I don't know what she expected from me. I had, after all, been divorced. The two people I loved more than my own life were gone for the most part. Nothing was as it was supposed to be or as I wanted it to be. I never asked for much but I sure wanted more than this. I guess she wanted me to give her the Jolly Time report and when I didn't, she walked away. I can't tell you how many times I had people duplicate this same scene with me. They say half of all marriages end in divorce. The other half of the people out there, who don't end up in divorce have no idea what it feels like. I learned a lot about empathy and how rare it is. There are many people who went the other way when I walked by. They didn't ask about Holly, or ask how I was doing. The questions they asked were superficial and even mystifying. I had been divorced about 8 months when people began to ask me if I was dating again. It never failed to astound me how very little people understood about a divorce breakup. This wasn't like being dumped in High school. This wasn't the death of your dog or losing your car keys. It wasn't like being fired from a job or losing the vote for class president. It wasn't something I was going to be bouncing back from anytime soon but it seemed everyone expected me to. In fact, they were shocked when I hadn't. The friends I had who did understand were mostly other divorcees, men and women who knew where I was in the process simply by looking in my eyes. They always knew what to say and frequently, it was nothing at all. They understood the value of calling me and asking me to go to a movie or to grab a burger or go watch a ballgame. Just hanging out, giving me the opportunity to speak and letting me decide whether I would or not. They were patient and kind and never grew weary of my tears or my pain. Because they had walked this same path, they knew at what mile marker I was, and they waited patiently for me to progress. Adding to my sadness in the first four years after my divorce was the fact that all of my best friends lived somewhere else. Jim Wilson was in Florida, Jim Freeman was in North Carolina, Greg St. Clair was in Phoenix, and my friend Mark Sterling, who I had grown up with and who was more a brother than anything, was back home in Delaware. They all had lives and obligations that precluded talking on the phone for any length of time. Besides, being a guy I didn't want to talk as much as I wanted to just be around them. I longed for the days of my twenties when Mark and I did virtually everything together. We had talked, since high school, of one day buying a large parcel of land, maybe 50 acres, and building homes for our families on it. We talked of our kids growing up together as we had. I missed his friendship so much during those days when it was apparent I had lost everything. No matter what was going on in the world, Mark and I had always had fun. I needed that now, but I found that life rolls on and even our best friends don't have the time we need them to give us. None of that was Mark's fault or anyone else's but it hurt none the less and it served to remind me that I was, in fact, a grown up now and I had some real grown up problems to face. The people who did me the most good, who helped me in the greatest fashion were once again my surrogate families, Bob and Cathy and their family and Poppa John and Jewell. They had found me all those years before, when I was such a lost soul, convinced of my unloveableness and believing only the worst about myself. They had loved me as one of their own and showed me what real family is. They never stopped loving me even when I doubted why they could. Even when my doubts put them to the test.

When Holly and I divorced, they had little to say about her at all. They asked if she was okay, showing impartial concern. She had been, after all, their daughter in law. She was Morgan's mom and they all considered Morgan their grandchild. What they did do for me was remind me that *I had not lost them*. Regardless of my situation, their love for me was intact and stronger than ever. I was welcome in their home as I had always been and there was always a hand to hold and a shoulder to cry on. That was what I needed most, a sense of some normalcy. I needed to go home to Cathy and Bobs' and eat some of his famous wild game dishes hear the stories about how he'd stalked whatever it was we were eating at the time. I needed to tease and laugh and be around people who *knew* me and understood how much I had changed. It felt wonderful, like old times even, to walk into John and Jewell's home without knocking, as I had always done, and sit at the table and talk to Pop about faded glory and future hopes. For those moments, I was okay again. The world couldn't penetrate the happy memories I had made with these folks and being with them again made me feel like there would be some happier times one day.

Once again, I was at a crossroads where I could have easily slipped into a despair that consumed me. Once again, as they had before, these two wonderful families opened their hearts, loved me, and saved my life. Without them, I don't know where I would be. With them, there was hope that something would be normal again someday. It was sad that my only refuge was so far away, but at least I had them as a refuge. They represented normalcy and in hindsight, that is what I needed, and what I think most men need in the aftermath of divorce. Not much remains of their familiar old life. Divorce takes physical, tangible things away, like houses and possessions. It also takes a toll on friendships. The friends Holly and I had in common were few because we hadn't been in Nashville very long. The ones we did have were very torn, as is always the case. They loved us both and they did not want to have to choose. In some cases the easy solution was simply to avoid us both, another casualty of this war. Because of this, we need some sort of familiarity to be restored. We need to anchor to something that won't move and we need a point from which to reset our compass and get our bearings and see where we are going next.

I don't know how many guys do what I did and seek out relationships from their past. I do know that two of my best friends went through divorce and they both sought me out during that time. We didn't do much except talk and keep each other company but looking back, and especially having gone through it myself, I realize they just wanted a few hours of familiarity and a safe harbor to put in for the night. Knowing I still had my family, friends, and they still loved me like they always did, had been enough to keep me sane. There wasn't really anything they could do to fix it, and they were wise enough to know that. They were also wise enough to know that I was reaching out to them to see if anyone else was going to give up on me as Holly had. I thank God eternally that the answer was a resounding no and they were there, ready to love me like before.

The End and The beginning

Although the end to the hard-line, fighting came December 1, 1999 when Holly and I got our divorce, the battle for my soul had just begun. I don't know how many times in those first years after my divorce, I would pick up the phone with the intention of calling a friend, only to put it back down again. I don't know how many times I went out on a Friday night with nowhere in mind to go and no one I wanted to see. I don't know how many thousands upon thousands of desperate thoughts swirled around in my aching heart with no one to help me sort through them. I would drive around town aimlessly or just stay home in the dark, and it was all the same. I wore the look of a man who had seen far too many emotional battles and couldn't forget the carnage. I was a crushed, broken, devastated spirit. There was no light in my eyes or spring in my step.

Sadly, I had seen this pain before. In April of 1996, my beloved other family experienced the tragic loss of their youngest daughter in a car accident. I flew home immediately to be with them. Walking into the kitchen the next morning, I hugged Cathy, and felt the heartbreak in her voice and in her hug. Then I saw Bob…instantly the saying; the "eyes are the windows to the soul" came to mind. I saw in Bob's eyes a man who was broken and who was in the middle of a loss and grief that words could not contain. To this day, they still can't. I can only describe the look in his eyes as the same way an animals eyes look when it dies. The life and the shine were gone. Of all the things that made me weep when Collette passed away, I think looking into Bob's eyes and seeing that empty, hollow pain was amongst the worst. I look at pictures of me in the years after my divorce and the same sort of hollowness is there in my eyes.

They say divorce is like death in many ways. I agree. I aged more in the next five or six years than any other period in my life. I couldn't sleep. I lost interest in everything that I used to love. Nothing brought me happiness except my daughter. Therefore, I got to be happy once a week and every other weekend. Every day in between was a blur of merely trying to survive. I couldn't concentrate at work and my production suffered. I was ashamed because I was now divorced. I couldn't look anyone in the eye, because I thought they were all judging me for being divorced. I read books on how to help your child adapt to divorce and what to look out for and what to expect for them, and the books scared me to death. Friends of mine would ask me how I was doing and I always said, *"I'm okay."* *"Okay?"* I wasn't okay, I was dying! I was so far gone I didn't know who I was anymore. I had lost everything I cared about and yet I was reflexively, telling people I was okay. I was a man, and men aren't supposed to hurt...even in my most intense pain I knew this. I could not admit to anyone that I was hurting. I figured they knew already and they didn't want to talk about it.

Deep down inside I was screaming for someone to come help me survive this mess. I missed my boyhood friends the most. I think it was because they represented the innocence I had now so completely lost. They were around me the last time I was happy and I missed the way that all felt. It amazed me the amount of bad advice I got during this time. Nobody wanted to get close enough to cry with me or close enough to get a good look at my wounds, but they had all the time in the world for shallow, anecdotal advice that wasn't worth the air they wasted speaking it. It's amazing how many people, church members included, were suddenly experts on my battle!

Suddenly the world was full of armchair marriage counselors who had all sorts of post-war advice to give about the battles, now that they were over. And, of course, the requisite, *"You know I never really liked Holly anyway"*...here's a bit of free advice...the next time someone you know gets a divorce, *never* say that. I loved her more than words could ever express and one piece of paper didn't change that. I was surprised at how shallow people were, and how shallow they expected me to be about this. They were essentially advising me that I should have the capacity to simply turn-off my love for my wife at will. What kind of man would that have made me? What kind of nonsense was that? Is that the best anyone could think of? *"I never liked her anyway"* or *"you're better off without her"* Are you serious. Take a good look at me! I have bags under my eyes from not sleeping for over a year now! I still cry myself to sleep most nights! I'm still wearing my wedding band after a year, for God's sake! Do I LOOK like I'm better off? Does the fact that you say you never liked her make me feel the slightest bit better? Do you think that will help me sleep tonight, having your permission to be better off without her? Are you willing to sit up with me until 3 A.M. while I weep for my daughter, miss my wife, and wait for sleep to come? Have you taken inventory of all you have, and then considered how much of *those same things I've lost?* Do that…then tell me how fast I should get over it, and how much better off I am. Consider all that I am expected to get over before you explain to me how fast this should happen.

Chapter 6

Someone Help me Cry

Once during the difficult days immediately following the passing of their daughter, my friends had gotten an article from the Compassionate Friends newsletter. (CF is a support group for families who have lost a child) One story told of a little boy who came home very late for dinner. His mom was grilling him about it and she said, *"Where were you?"* The boy replied, *"Johnny and I were riding bikes and his bike broke down and I stayed to help him"* His mom replied, *"help him?"* *"You can't fix a bike, what do you mean you stayed to help him?"* The little boy replied, *"I know I can't fix a bike mom, I was helping him cry."* That story broke my heart. The writer was trying to say that words and deeds weren't always necessary. In fact, many times they are harmful. The simple, yet daring and vulnerable act of weeping with me was what I needed. I needed a man to pray with me and a man who was comfortable enough to let me cry in front of him. And how I needed to cry!

I missed my wife so much those first years. Every song was a reminder. Every little, silly thing. She had left many belongings at my house and every time I discovered something of hers that she had forgotten, it was breaking my heart all over again. You want to know what you miss when you lose your wife and your family to divorce. *Everything.* I missed the way she stole the covers in the night. I missed the way she stayed in the shower until the hot water was gone. I missed the way she made tuna salad. I missed the sound of her voice and the smell of her perfume and the feeling of her next to me in the night. I missed all the stupid music she liked that I couldn't stand, and the way she'd roll her eyes when I'd crank up the Springsteen, and I missed her watching "Friends" while I snuck out of the room because I couldn't bear it. I missed the knowing in my soul that she was home with me.

Believe me when I tell you, no matter what you think your wife does that annoys you, no matter what habits of hers you think you can live without, and no matter how much better off you think you'll be, someday, somehow, You will miss her. It will hit you in an unguarded moment and you will be undone, and it does not matter what she might have done to you in your entire life together, you will miss her. I missed my wife. And she wasn't coming back, and I couldn't talk about it with anyone because nobody knew how, and nobody thought they really needed to learn. Regardless of this fact, it seemed like everyone expected me to set a time limit on my sorrow and *"move on."*

Boy…there is a phrase I could do with never hearing again. People would throw that out there and not even think about it. Move on. Move on from what, exactly? Have you ever considered that? I had a wife that I love, I have a beautiful daughter that I adore, and my sole desire in life is to see her grow up healthy and happy. Being married was how I defined myself and my happiness. You know…you are right! I should move on from all that! It should be easy. The real fact, looking back on those people who would say that, was that they were too uncomfortable seeing my grief and too darned selfish to want to step into it to help. Compassion and empathy are such rare commodities these days. What I needed was someone who was willing to just sit and listen, or even just sit in silence with me. Perhaps go to a movie or a ball game, or doing anything that resembled normalcy. We didn't have to discuss the divorce every time. I just needed someone to listen whenever I *did* want to discuss it. But nobody ever asked or offered and I suffered through all my "flashbacks" and nightmares alone and in silence.

There was a couple I knew who were in ministry together. They had been friends of mine for a few years and had gotten to know Holly a little after we moved to Nashville. They were aware of the situation and never once did they call or reach out in any way. I lived less than a mile from their house and I never heard a peep from them...until, of course, they were moving and needed some help loading a truck. I might have been a sorrowful reclusive divorcee, but I was a big and strong sorrowful reclusive divorcee, and while they ignored me in my pain, they called me in their need. It's no wonder vets all hang out together at the VFW or the Legion post. Maybe in addition to being the only people who understand them, they are the only ones who *care*.

One of the great tragedies of the Church is our expectation that everyone is, or should be, on the same plane spiritually that we are. I think that maybe everyone I knew in the church had a preconceived notion about how I should have been dealing with my sorrow. Maybe in their minds, they thought I was "naming the Name" and "giving it to God" and there was no need to reach out to me. I was giving it to God all right! Their hair would have straightened if they had heard me doing it. Maybe they didn't know what to say. Maybe the thought my divorce would somehow rub off on their marriage. Maybe I reminded them too much of where they were headed. I also think it was some serious judgment occurring. I think people were subconsciously shunning me because "God hates divorce." I think it's safe to say this was not what I needed. I already felt like I was condemned. I felt like I was a failure, I worried that my daughter would become a statistic, I dreaded the thoughts that my wife was going to start dating someday soon, I felt useless and washed up. I did not need anyone else helping me feel this way.

There was one more thing…I really think people were afraid to reach out to me because I might cry. I wonder, what is so frightening about a weeping man? Women cry in church all the time. They cry in restaurants and doctors offices. They cry on trains and buses and behind the wheel of their own cars. But have you ever seen a man weeping loudly at church? What is your reaction? What is the reaction of the people around you? It draws attention doesn't it? It is an oddity. And I think it's somehow scary to people. A wailing woman is okay and should be comforted; a sobbing man is a lunatic. Why? Why are we expected to keep it together when we just lost it all? I am not talking about men giving up the Y chromosome, and getting all metrosexual. I am talking about a man honestly weeping at the darkest moment of his life.

I wonder what the reaction of modern day men would have been to a weeping Jesus when Lazarus died. How fast would we have run the other direction if we saw Him coming at us undone in His sorrow and grief? That model of Christ will close this section, in the form of a plea. Please…the next time you are in church and you see a man who is going through or has gone through a divorce, reach out to him. The next time you hear of someone going through it, find his number, and call him, and more than that, go and find him! In fact, I pray you will take on the mantle of Jesus' example here and you will look into the man's heart, see his ache and his pain, and weep with him. I dare you! More than that, I beg you! Come up to me, sit down next to me, look into my eyes, tell me you understand and your heart is breaking with mine, and tell me its okay to weep, by weeping with me! Your arm around my shoulder and the tears in your eyes tell me more than any words you could say. Right now, at this moment, I don't even want to think about answers. My heart isn't finished it's breaking yet and I have a river of tears in me. You can make a real difference in my life and cry some of them with me, or you can hide from me because you are uncomfortable, or you feel inadequate and in doing so, condemn me to crying them alone. Either way I will cry, you can count on it. Whether my soul is ministered to as it empties out is up to you. What goes into the vacuum created by my marriage being ripped apart depends largely on what those around me do to help fill the void.

Please, take a minute; imagine yourself going home to emptiness tonight. Imagine tucking your kids in by telephone, and sleeping alone. Imagine you just lost the very things that got you up and out of bed every morning. Now find the tears in your heart and weep with me! One of my favorite movies is "I am Legend." I was a fan of "The Omega Man" with Charlton Heston when I was a kid. "I Am Legend" is a remake of that same story, (Which was, in fact, a remake of an earlier version of the novel) As good as Heston's portrayal of Robert Neville was; Will Smith was even better. One scene defines the crushing loneliness I felt in the early years of my post-divorce life. Smiths' character, Dr. Robert Neville is the last man left alive in New York City. As far as he knows, he is the last man on earth. The only creatures alive are wild animals, his dog Samantha, and the nocturnal mutants left by the cancer vaccine that went horribly wrong and caused the annihilation of the human race.

After a horrific battle with some of the mutants and their mutant pit bulls, Neville's dog Sam dies in his arms. She was his only companionship and the next day he goes to a video store, as he was apt to do each day. His routine on these trips to the video store included carrying on mock conversation with some mannequins he had placed in the store and named. Until this scene, these "conversations" were tongue in cheek, mostly him making light of his lack of any companionship other than Sam. However, in this scene, Sam is dead and he goes to the store and wanders inside lost and dazed. He walks up to a mannequin and says *"hello"*...only this time his voice is quivering and he is far more serious. The crushing loneliness and realization that his only companion is gone is overwhelming and Neville begins to weep and repeat the desperate request... *"Please...PLEASE say hello to me..."* He leaves the store in tears because he knows no response is coming and he is all alone.

When I saw that scene for the first time, I wept in the darkness of the theatre. I was that same man in that same situation for so long. My heart ached and I felt like I had lost every human that I knew. My companion was gone and I was in a daze and in shock and my heart wanted to cry out to anyone who would answer... *"Please. Please just say hello to me."* If you are reading this book for insight into the heart of a divorced man...there it is. Most of us are, or were in this position. This is how we feel. We have lost our companion, our familiar surroundings, our love, and we feel like the last isolated man on the planet in a world full of hateful, soul eating mutants lurking in the shadows. We feel strange and different and we really need to feel like we belong. So with that in mind...when you see one of us in your midst...Please...just say hello.

Flashbacks and Nightmares

One interesting lesson I have learned in the 13 years since my divorce, is how there is always something lurking around every corner to trigger memories. Maybe its memories of something you and your wife once did together, or just the sudden reminder during the day that you are, in fact, divorced. Now I admit I am an emotional guy, so maybe these things are triggered in me more easily than in other men. But I don't think I'm very different. Memory prompts cannot be controlled sometimes. It's silly really. My favorite story? Okay, imagine this; I'm grocery shopping in Publix one day a few years ago and not paying much attention and suddenly I find myself listening to the background music playing over the loudspeakers. Who listens to Muzak, right? It's Sting and Toby Keith singing *"I'm so Happy That I Can't Stop Crying."* (Maybe the best song about men in divorce ever written) Suddenly, as I am listening to the words, I am in tears. Now, I am 6' 4" and so there is no effective way to hide my weeping in a grocery store. So I abandon my cart and make my way to the produce section where the aisles are wider and I can blend in. I tried to hide behind the melons. Listening to those two men singing right then was too much. I was thrust back to December 1, 1999, and I could see my wife in court, leaving without me. I felt all the same feelings again…

Seven weeks have passed now since she left me,
She shows her face to ask me how I am
She says the kids are fine and that they miss me
Maybe I could come and baby-sit sometime

This was too much…the sadness of hearing a man talk about the seven weeks that have passed. I marked those days on my calendar too. I knew too well the feeling of coming home each night to the echoing emptiness of a house without my family, and I too, marked each day in my mind and in my heart. Day one…week three…it's been three months….I knew what Sting was really saying here. I buried my face in my hands, acting as if I had something in my eye, so at least I had an excuse for my tears…

The park is full of Sunday fathers and melted ice cream

We try to do the best within the given time

A kid should be with his mother, everybody knows that

What can a father do but baby-sit sometimes?

I'm so happy that I can't stop crying

I'm laughing through my tears…

I think it was the park being full of "Sunday fathers" that broke my heart all over again. My thoughts ran to my little girl and to how much I missed her. I remember one night right after Holly and I divorced, maybe only two weeks or so, I called her to talk to Morgan and say good night. I was telling Morgan I loved her and I was so overcome with sadness and emotion that I sort of collapsed on the floor of my hallway and sobbed into the phone, telling her over and over how much I loved her. I wanted to hold my precious little girl in my arms, and smell her soft baby powder smell and brush her long golden curls with my hands and tuck her in, but I had to do it over the phone. At that moment, it was too much. Fatherhood reminds me of my situation all the time. I have wanted to be a dad since I can remember. When I was a little boy my favorite show was "The Courtship of Eddies Father" only I wanted to be both Eddie and Tom Corbett. I always saw myself becoming a dad one day. I coached high school ice hockey for seven years before I was married. I took every one of those young men to heart and I was a father figure for many of them. Let me tell you something, you don't turn off your "daddy mode"…ever. I see my daughter once a week and every other weekend, and yet I worry about her as if she was with me every second. You want to know my personal definition of divorce hell. Here is a snapshot from my life… I live on the edge of "Tornado Alley" here in Nashville. We aren't hit with nearly the same frequency as they do in Oklahoma or Texas or Arkansas, but every spring we have a stretch of a month or so where the warnings are buzzing every few days, and we have had some major twisters here. One night I am awakened by the sound of approaching thunder and I turn on my TV to see the local news weatherman interrupting some late-night show to warn the area of impending storms coming our way. More precisely, they are heading straight for the part of town where my ex wife and my daughter were living at the time. I tried to call her but it went straight to voice mail. If you want to know what powerlessness feels like, try being a daddy, and having a daddy's protective heart and warrior spirit, and not being able to protect your little girl in a time of danger. Those tears, my friends, are the most bitter of all. It was hours before I was able to tell from the local news coverage, that the storms had missed her neighborhood and they were okay. Each spring, for the past nine years, I have spent agonizing nights on my knees. Each long, seemingly endless night, crying and praying that God would do what I could not do and protect my daughter.

The things many men take for granted, are the things I treasure most. Tucking her in at night, saying prayers together. Making pancakes on Saturday morning. Teaching her to make my grandmothers spaghetti sauce. Going for walks around the neighborhood and talking about the moon, the stars, and her dreams for her life. Try doing that only 4 nights a month. I hear men complain about child support all the time…there are things that are taken from you in divorce that have nothing to do with money. Each weekend ends with me taking a slightly panicked inventory of the previous 48 hours. *"Did I do enough with her?" "Did I spend enough time talking with her… does she know how much I love her…did I increase her faith and did she have a good time?" "Could I have done anything differently?"* I am on a never-ending treadmill of self-examination because the time limits we face, force me to try to squeeze 14 days worth of fatherhood into 58 hours. That task is nearly impossible.

Here is another memory prompt. My friend told me she saw her son do this once and sure enough, not long after that it happened to me. My daughter had a school assembly in third grade. Holly and her new husband showed up and were seated in the audience left of the stage. I sat to the right. Morgan did her performance and then when it was done, the parents were invited back to the homeroom for snacks and socializing. Morgan came down off the stage and she saw me, then she saw her mom on the other side of the room, and I could see the dilemma creep across her little face. "Which one do I run to first?" She was caught in the middle without asking to be. I quickly mouthed the words to her "go see your mom" and I could see the relief. I walked over and stood about ten feet away, like Naaman the leper, until Holly let her come over and spend a few minutes with me. If I had forgotten, during the course of the day, that I was divorced, that scene surely brought me back to reality.

There are many other ways...like having to call your child's teacher to ask for a copy of her report card, because she doesn't live with you and you didn't see that last one. Or when the school pictures come out and nobody remembered to send you some of the proofs and an order form, and you don't have any pictures in your wallet because nobody thought about you. One last thing...this one hurts and I have used this analogy many times with friends of mine. You never forget you are divorced because your time with your children is defined and specific. Men who are not in this situation take this for granted. I can tell you that every other weekend when I pick Morgan up for our visit, I can feel the clock running like a meter on a cab the very second she gets in my truck. From Friday after school until 6pm Sunday evening, it feels like that. It's like being a prisoner because it's so structured. My friends can always tell when I have had her for a weekend, because I am miserable for about half the day on Monday because I miss her so much. The summer visit is much worse. I tell people that on June 1, when she comes to my house for the summer, I feel like I am Dorothy in the wizard of Oz. In the scene where the witch gives her until the hourglass runs out to hand over the ruby slippers. No matter what Dorothy does, or how she turns over the hourglass, the sand keeps on running out. From June 1 to August 1 each summer, I am Dorothy. I am Capt. Hook and I can hear a clock ticking somewhere. The first week of August, I usually take off a few days and go hide. It takes a lot out of you to get "back to normal" when what you just had for two months is normal. Missing your children is a hurt that never feels better. And the restrictions all but eliminate doing anything spontaneous with them. You can't just take them away for a surprise weekend vacation without clearing it with their mother first. These are things that don't get mentioned when you meet with your attorney.

Chapter 7

*...And You Can't Take
That From Me*

This is a difficult chapter to write…

Difficult to write about, difficult to think about and revisit, but it needs to be addressed because virtually every divorced man will go through it at some point. The day you realize your wife found someone else and she really isn't coming back.

I had been holding out hope for reconciliation for years. Holly dated some but it never seemed to last for her. Holly was dating almost immediately after our divorce. She was involved with a young resident at the hospital where she worked, and then she dated a guy she worked with in a different practice. She dated another guy I had known while I lived here, before she and I had ever met. He was a real scumball and it didn't end well for either of them. After that guy, she didn't date for a while, and I hoped we'd somehow work things out. I was still very much in love with her and would have done anything she desired in order to win her back.

We worked together very well when it came to Morgan. Birthdays, Christmas, Preschool events. We did all of those things for Morgan's sake and in my heart, I had hoped she would see how good it could be and want to give us another try. She would call me when she needed something repaired on her car or something fixed in her apartment. I allowed her to do this, which was a huge mistake, and I never said no. I was setting myself up for a horrible crash. She didn't want me back, but she liked me being around to take care of things like fixing a flat or jumping a battery. I was a useful idiot, as Stalin once said, but in my mind all the inclusion was a sign that there was still hope.

I should have known better, and looking back of course, I do now. In reality, I played myself for a fool. I kept chugging along; hoping that these times of coexistence would lead to reconciliation because I was so much in love with her. I couldn't even picture a life without her. The possibility didn't even exist in my mind.

Then one day she had a date with the guy she ended up marrying. He was a pharmaceutical salesman and knew how to impress her. He sent flowers to her office. Their first date was a lavish dinner at a local restaurant known for its elegance and high priced menu. A limo arrived to pick her up and whisk her off for a romantic evening…with a doctor friend of his and the doctors wife. If I questioned his motives, she defended him in anything he did and I sensed I was in trouble. He tried asserting his presence in her life more and more, and I kept trying to reveal how very average he was. I was jealous and this was stupid, but I had never been on this ground before and did what a lot of guys do…I thought I could talk her out of it. None of this mattered to her at all. She defended him blindly. That was different for her. Something inside me sank, and I knew this was *the* guy. This guy was going to ruin my chances to have my wife back.

I lost sight of the fact that for him, this was also the woman of *his* dreams. He didn't understand how much I still loved her and he, having never been married before, didn't consider my feelings in the matter. He also can be a bit arrogant, as salesmen are who find success, he is a type A personality and needs to dominate any situation, and he sensed my concerns over it. He relished the chance to make my life miserable, and he did so every chance he got.

The highlight of my interactions with him was one evening in June of 2002. Holly and I had been arguing because she wasn't buckling Morgan into her booster seat and I was concerned she would get hurt. Her boyfriend called me, and began to inform me that, although they had been dating only 3 months at the time, he was going to marry her and when Holly and Morgan were at his house it was *"none of your damned business"* what happened with my daughter. He then started to tell me how he was going to be Morgan's "new daddy" and I had better just get used to it. He was telling me how he had started a college fund for my daughter, (after dating her mother for 3 months…do I even need to comment here?), and he was going to be better at it than I was.

Well…Jackpot! He had hit a homerun. He left no base uncovered and no stone unturned. He lead off with his pronouncement of his intentions to marry the woman I still loved, and then he told me he was supplanting me as Morgan's' father. He had peed on every tree and marked his turf. He should have spit on my grandmother too and gotten the hat trick. I went insane. I was barely intelligible in my response but I did manage to spit out *"who do you think you are starting a college fund for my daughter? You'd better take that money and get a good life insurance policy for yourself pal because when I'm done with you the dogs won't even know where to start looking for your bones!"* I can't even recall what I said after that but it was probably the most rage-fueled outpouring I had ever uttered.

Outwardly, I was one really angry Italian from Philly…but inside, my heart sank…what if this was true? What if they were going to get married? What if Holly let him take my place as Morgan's daddy? Holly had already revealed her penchant for causing me pain. She seemed eerily happy when I suffered. And this was making me suffer beyond what I could bear. I called her the next day and asked her what on earth that was all about. How could she let someone tell me I was going to be replaced? I told her I was always going to defend her motherhood where Morgan was concerned and I hoped she would do the same for me. But she remained strangely silent and told me repeatedly how Morgan "loved" this man. I believe, in her mind she wouldn't have cared if he replaced me completely. She seemed to be enjoying twisting this particular knife because she knew how it hurt me.

I was crushed. I was now losing the woman I adored and it seemed my daughter as well. I have never been as scared as I was then. If I lost my daughter, I would die. I had not yet learned the truth about being a dad and I was consumed by fear and by another man's presence in my daughter's life. Holly and Jeff essentially moved in together not long after that. He spent at least four nights at her house each week. I could have gone to court and put a stop to it but I decided to try to keep the peace. I was more lost than ever by that point. I was on the Titanic watching the last lifeboat pulling away as the waters rushed toward me, and I was too dumbfounded to know what to do to survive.

About a year later, she showed up to drop off Morgan to me, and Holly was wearing a large engagement ring. I complimented her on the ring and tried to hide my heartache. He was, that same day, signing the papers for a new house he was buying for them. They had set a date for the following year. I went home and cried. Then I threw up. I couldn't even speak the words that she was going to remarry. I felt like my world was in a thousand pieces and each piece was slipping through my fingers. Each time I tried to pick up one, I would drop two more. What little was remaining of my heart, broke that day. To top it off, she informed me that he had also bought Morgan a tiny diamond ring. I don't know what he thought it signified. I have seen guys do that but generally in situations where the child's father is not in the picture either by death or by abandonment. Holly should have told him this was inappropriate, but she let him intrude even further on my sacred ground. This was his way of again marking his turf, and it was going to have a very ugly conclusion unless he backed down.

They set a wedding date for May of 2004. I remember the date, not because she told me and I wrote it down, but because they left right after Morgan's graduation from Kindergarten. I can't forget that night because for one thing, the event was so special, and for another thing, Holly's fiancé broke into my car in the parking lot and stole a cordless drill from my trunk. He was that kind of a guy.

The day they got married, I went to a restaurant and watched a hockey game. The Flyers were in the playoffs and I needed the diversion. Then I did what I had never done before and bought a bottle of Jack Daniels. I thought maybe drinking would make me feel something other than the immense pain and hollow gaping hole I had in my chest. I went home, opened the bottle, and took a slug. I decided right then I wasn't going to let them get the best of me and do something I wouldn't normally do so I poured the bottle down the drain. I went to bed instead.

When I woke up the next day, I felt different somehow. I wasn't as sad as I thought I would be. I was strangely relieved. She was married. It was over now. She was never coming back and I would never again be tormented with that false hope. There was sadness but also a finality that felt a little lighter. I could finally allow myself to go to whatever the next stage was going to be because this one was over. To be honest, I was so exhausted from the four years of trying to win her back and the way that just played into her hands, that I needed a rest. I was still very worried about my fatherhood. That was still threatened, at least in my eyes.

About a week later I found out that was intact and could never be challenged, although the way this was revealed was through a betrayal. Morgan came to my house for the weekend and I asked her about the wedding. I did not do it because I wanted details, honestly I couldn't have cared less. Morgan needed to know that she could talk to me about anything and that included something she knew would hurt me. So I asked her how her mommy looked and what dresses did they wear and what flowers did she carry? She gave me a description and then she said something that cut me to the bone. She said, *"Mommy is changing her last name to Jeff's last name but I'm not going to"* I asked her if she thought she could do that and she said, *"Mommy asked me if I wanted to change my name to Jeff's name but I said no."* As angry as I was at that moment, I hid it from her and asked her why she didn't want to change it. She looked at me incredulous and said, *"Because you are my daddy, not Jeff. Mommy said I could call him whatever I wanted to and I told her I wanted to call him Jeff because I didn't want to call anyone else Daddy but you"* I hugged her as tightly as I ever had. I realized something that took me almost 2 years to understand...I was her *daddy*! I was doing it right and he had absolutely no shot against a love like the love I have for my daughter, because she knew I loved her.

From that day on, neither he nor Holly could ever bother me quite the way they had before. The one thing I cared most about losing was never going anywhere and there wasn't anything those two could do about it. In the end, it wasn't Holly who would protect my fatherhood; it was me. I was a great dad, I loved my daughter, and she knew it. That bond could not be broken or even strained, unless by my hand. I wasn't going anywhere or doing anything to cause harm to that precious relationship.

Holly and Jeff lost control of me that day, and I found that the one unconditional love I could cling to back then was still intact. Another little sign that maybe I'd survive this thing. I want to state here that I wish the animosity wasn't permanent, at least not for Holly and me. That's how it has to be. Divorce is stressful enough for the kids without palpable stress between the parents. I have bitten my tongue and held my peace on many occasions. I have not been perfect, I admit, but I want Morgan to love her Mom and respect her. Any decisions she makes concerning her feelings about the divorce should be dealt with when she gets older. I want her to still have a childhood and not bear the burden of all this and not allow it to make her grow up too fast. I retained the best thing our marriage produced…the love of my daughter and the privilege of being her dad. That can't be stripped from me and for that I am thankful.

Chapter 8

Where Did All This Pain Come from?

That seems like a ridiculous question…

…I mean this is a book about divorce from a man's perspective and you would think that, unless I am writing from a pro-divorce viewpoint, nobody would be questioning whether this hurt or not. Nevertheless, I have been asked quite frequently why, considering how unhappy we both were, considering the acrimony before, during, and after the divorce, why did it hurt so much?

That is without a doubt a personal issue. I doubt any two men deal with it the same way. It depends on a million factors and because I am not writing a textbook, I didn't research anyone else's besides my own. My own reasons are sufficient for the conversation at hand and maybe they will prompt the reader to investigate his own handling of his grief. I have met men who handled divorce with undaunted aplomb. It was no more upsetting or discomforting than a minor traffic accident. The kids will be fine, we are better friends now than when we were married, and I have more time for golf. Nothing hurts them and nothing dents the carapace of denial and incredible selfishness with which they surround themselves.

These were typically the guys who had the most advice to offer, whether I asked for it or not. I found most of them to be excruciatingly self-centered, considering neither the pain of their children or their ex spouse, nor their own sorrow…no matter how far beneath the surface it lay. Some of them were truly without remorse or sadness. Those were the men I understood the least. The ones who were so quick to tell me how my daughter was going to be just fine and kids are resilient. It was as if the faster they could get those words out of their mouths the sooner they could squelch the screaming guilt inside their own hearts. So why, in this world of 6 month grieving periods for most guys, did I drag this pain around for over 6 years? Why so many nights of tears and sorrow and days of endless, aimless drifting? What was lurking inside me that missed marriage so much that even a bad one ending would ruin me? What hole did I have in me that I had expected marriage to fill? Those were some of the questions I wrestled with for years. I didn't even realize I was wrestling for a long time.

It took eight years after my divorce to realize my sorrow was coming from some holes not created by the dissolution of my marriage. Since as early as I can remember I wanted to be married. As far back as I can recall I saw myself as a husband and a father. It took a while but I came to understand this in the years after my divorce. I don't know if everyone is like me but I have oftentimes in my life, found healing for wounds in my soul by recreating the environment that wounded me, and then hoping my environment heals instead of hurts. I grew up in a loveless, graceless home. I cannot recall ever once resting in unconditional love as a child. In fact, the last time I remembered feeling unconditional love was when we lived with my grandmother, before my mother married my stepfather. When she married him and we moved away, nothing was the same. We had little in common and he rarely showed the slightest interest in me. Growing up thinking he was my natural father only made this worse. I saw his rejection of me as a reflection of my value as a person...not as the lack of bond between a man and his wife's son. If he rejected me, it surely was because I was unlovable and that was my fault.

This environment fostered a strong desire in me for marriage. I think I had created an image of how I wished my home could be and, having realized that was never going to happen, I convinced myself that I would one day create that life in my own marriage. Being a husband and a dad would somehow fill all those holes and heal all those wounds that my childhood had inflicted. I didn't know any of this going in...I just thought I was meant to be a husband.

What this did to me was twofold. First it put an enormous amount of pressure on me to actually succeed in marriage from day one. I had no real family to speak of and so if this failed, I had nothing. The tragedy there was that it put ridiculous pressure on Holly to respond to me, as I needed her to. When she did not, it became much more of a problem than it should have. My entire identity was contained in my marriage and nobody should have been put under that kind of stress. I needed to prove myself by being a flawless husband and I could not be. Nobody can.

Because Holly too was flawed, she never saw that part of me and when I failed, as all men will do, instead of love and grace she met it with ridicule and personal attack. That only fed my emptiness and need even more, and it all snowballed out of control. I hope men reading this book will spend some time here. Look deep within yourselves and find out what it is that may be causing you to put an undo amount of expectation on your marriage. Are you looking to your wife and children for the kind of confirmation that you need to be getting from God alone? Are there holes in your heart and wounds in your soul that you brought into this thing, and now you are realizing that you've expected someone else to fill and heal them for you? Someone not equipped for that work?

One of the good things that have been born from this divorce has been the realization that I have to find my healing and fulfillment in Christ. I have to get to where I know who God says I am and I believe it to be true. Only then can I enter into any relationship complete, healthy, and truly ready to give my all and not have my happiness determined by the response of my spouse.

Going through life unnoticed

Let me make it clear...I don't care for chick flicks. Nevertheless, occasionally there is a gem buried beneath the Kleenex boxes. I was watching a movie on TV one day and found an entire chapter buried in the midst of one such girl movie. The movie was called "Shall we Dance" ...not the Yul Brenner version but a different movie that starred Richard Gere and Susan Sarandon and Jennifer Lopez. I won't even bother going into the plot...it is incidental to this story.

Now normally I would instantly change the channel if I even catch a glimpse of Gere or Sarandon...especially Sarandon. But the movie was interesting and Jennifer Lopez is a stunning woman and I had time to kill. Well, one scene moved me deeply and it explained perfectly why marriage mattered to me so much. Susan Sarandon is explaining to a friend, why she is sure her husband (Gere) is not cheating on her. She explains her theory on why people get married. She says it is to avoid going unnoticed. She then makes the following astounding soliloquy.

"People get married because they don't want to go unnoticed. There are 6 Billion people in the world and it is so easy to get lost in a crowd that size. Getting married and having a spouse means there is someone else in that crowd who can say *I see you...you aren't just a nameless face in the crowd and your being here has been noticed.*"

That is a paraphrase, but it is the part I remember and it effected me deeply. In a 1985 book called "Glory Days...Bruce Springsteen in the 80's" one chapter dealt with Bruce's decision to get married at age 34. He had said that during a prolonged time off the road, during the recording and release of the "Nebraska" album, he had begun to open himself up to his neighbors and friends. He had been somewhat reclusive until that stage of his life and now he found himself calling his neighbors over for cookouts and softball games. He also was spending more time with his married sister and her family. He realized this was something missing in his life.

Not long after, he attended the wedding of Marc Brickman, Bruce's longtime lighting director. The rabbi made a statement during the wedding that Bruce claims touched him deeply. He said, "A man spends his life dreaming dreams, hoping hopes and making plans. When he takes a wife, when he finds that one person to spend his life with, he takes his first step towards making his dreams come true" Bruce claims it was that line that really convinced him of his desire for lifetime companionship. He often quoted the wonderful "It Takes Two" by Marvin Gaye and Kim Weston as another source for his viewpoint of marriage.

I have to agree. I came from this school of thought. My wife was my witness. She was the one person who was going to be there at the end, reminding me that I was really here and I mattered. She was going to be the person who reinforced my belief in myself when I was down, and who would reel me in when I got carried away. We would one day look back on a lifetime together and wonder at what a crazy, marvelous, rocky, twisting, turning, zigging and zagging ride it had been. And we would walk off together into our sunset years, satisfied that we had both borne witness to each other's validity. We would grow old gracefully, knowing that we had left an indelible, wonderful imprint on each other and our children. 50 years, 60 years…maybe more. We would one day look back and realize that without the other, none of this would have amounted to anything. The rough times bore the fruit of good times and the tears watered the fertile soil that brought forth smiles and happiness.

One of my favorite all-time movies is "Saving Private Ryan." The most touching scene to me is at the very end…Private Ryan has been visiting Normandy with his wife and extended family. The entire movie is his recollection of that terrible battle, and the squad of soldiers who gave all to find him and bring him home after losing all of his brothers. Captain Miller, the squad leader, (played by Tom Hanks) has been shot and is mortally wounded. Realizing this is his dying moment; he grabs the young Private Ryan and says, "Earn this." Young Ryan can't quite hear him so he leans forward and Miller reaches up and grabs him by his jacket and says, "James…earn this" He realized he, and most of his other men had given their very lives to bring him home safely. He wanted his sacrifice to be meaningful and he implored his young charge to live his life in tribute to the great price that had been paid. The final scene is the now elderly James Ryan, looking at the white marble cross bearing the name of that same Captain Miller who gave his life and who charged him with so sobering a command. Ryan turns to his wife and with tears in his eyes, he asks desperately… "Have I been a good man?" "Tell me I've lived a good life!" He counted on the one person who walked with him every step, from the first vows to the final goodbyes, to assure him he kept his promise to his fallen comrades. Whom else would he ask? Your spouse knows you better, for longer, than anyone else in the world. They know things about you that your best friends or your parents don't know and never will.

I had dreamed a dream and planned a plan. The completion of this plan depended on Holly being there at the end, reassuring me that my time on earth was not in vain, I had "Lived a good life", and I was a "good man." Not in the eternal sense, of course, that confirmation comes only from God, but from the sense of my spouse, my best friend. Someone who walked every step with me and who could finally say, at the end… "I am proud of the way you carried yourself all these years." And hopefully, "I would gladly have walked them again with you." That is gone for me now, and gone for many other men like me.

I don't know if I'll ever allow someone into that part of my heart and soul again. Failure in that dark recess really makes it hard to bring it to light again. That is another thing that made it so hard to let go, and made it hurt so much. All I had now was the confirmation that I did not do well. I was not a good man. She did not want to go through it with me to the very end. It hurt me to my core. Part of this desperate desire for affirmation needs to be resolved within the bounds of my faith, but part of it is meant to be provided through marriage. Otherwise, Adam would not have needed Eve.

Adam was a perfect man in a perfect place. We know that he walked with God physically everyday and spoke to Him at length. Yet this perfect man in a perfect world still needed completion. He needed a helper…not a physical helper; God could do all that for Adam. But he needed a helper for his heart and a companion. We all do. And when we lose that person before our journey ends it leaves a hole so large that sometimes it never is filled. It was eight years later before I could even begin contemplating the possibility of someone else taking that role in my life. It was perhaps the hardest thing to let go of. The release of dreams and hopes and the acceptance of the possibility that it might be someone else seeing those dreams come true is difficult. But in all honesty, it's really so vital for us.

When I have a bad day, I come home to no one. Nobody cares and nobody is there to tell me *"I know you, I believe in you, and I know tomorrow will be better."* There is no one there to celebrate with me when I have a success. Nobody to greet me with a hug and tell me *"I never doubted you for a minute...I knew you had this greatness inside you, I saw it from day one."* For me, there is only quiet and aloneness.

I had hoped that my marriage might declare my existence in a way my childhood and my homelife could not. I had not achieved the lofty goals I had set out to achieve years before, and so I hoped a successful marriage might be my legacy. Sadly, this failed as well. The last, best hope I had for identity and the one thing I thought might separate me from all my failures, instead became my ultimate failing. Now I was a faceless stranger...one-half of just another of the 50% of failed marriages in this country. Another weekend father and ex husband. The one source of unfailing love and unconditional acceptance I thought I might have was gone now too.

Maybe those signals I had been getting since childhood were right. Maybe I really was unlovable and unacceptable. Maybe I really couldn't do anything right in this life. Even something as natural to me as being a father, was being stripped from me. Some foreboding, dark abyss was calling my name and I felt destined to disappear into it. Destined to become just another nameless, faceless shadow dweller, who long ago lost the light in his eyes and the spring in his step. A man without a purpose in a vast sea of drifting, purposeless men. The only thing I really cared about and wanted to live for was gone and once again…as had seemed evident for as long as I could remember…nobody wanted me.

I had been set up for this since my earliest days, or so it seemed. The message was never vague… "You aren't anything to be desired." That's what I had heard in my soul since I was a kid. I took that right into my marriage and then watched it morph into a self-fulfilling prophecy. Lacking anything resembling self-confidence where relationships were concerned, I imploded almost instantly, once the difficulties started. Unconditional love was a foreign subject to me and so I dreaded Holly leaving me long before she ever began to threaten it. I felt like I was over my head from day one with her. I kept right on behaving as if I was on borrowed time. The lack of unconditional love can inspire anger like few know. Fear inspires anger too. I lived in a constant state of fear that Holly would leave me. It began to influence my decision making almost immediately.

Long before the arguments began, the fear was already screaming in my ears. The Bible says, "Out of the abundance of the heart, the mouth speaks," and the abundance I carried in my heart was that of fear and doubt. It spoke in reactions to Holly and to situations that a healthy view wouldn't have tolerated. I was doomed before I began, but I never realized it.

I know this is true for so many divorced folks. They look back and realize the things that torpedoed their marriage were not new to the relationship. They were carry-on baggage that they either didn't know they had or never saw how large those issues were. The unspoken code is we all expect to marry someone "healthy" and "adjusted." We live with that lurking in our minds and hold ourselves up to unrealistic expectations almost immediately in the marriage. There is no rest in that relationship, only performance driven madness.

Chapter 9

People Let Me Tell You
'Bout My Best Friend

It is obvious to anyone reading by now...

...that my daughter is the sum total of my world. She is the axis upon which my world revolves and the light of my life. I could not wait to be a dad and for me, fatherhood began the day I found out Holly was expecting. I had always...for as long as I could remember... wanted to be a dad. I mean going back as far as when I was eight or nine. I longed to bond with a child of my own. Looking back it is easy to see why now. I was so very rejected and so very hurting for my dad that I created this picture of the perfect father / child relationship and put myself in both roles. In my imagination, I would become the perfect dad...and thereby finally have the dad I always wanted...even if by proxy.

When Holly found out she was pregnant I was scared for about 24 hours. The next morning I was ecstatic! Then we had the first ultrasound done and it hit me again...a second wave of incredible love and expectation and anticipation. As far as I was concerned I was already a daddy...I was just waiting to meet her face to face. I would talk to Holly's belly every night through a paper towel tube. One night, when Holly was about seven months pregnant, we were lying in bed and I leaned over and said *"Hi Morgan...it's your Daddy...I love you"*. Months of talking to her that way resulted in her recognizing my voice and she kicked and moved in Holly's belly. We both laughed until we cried. My little girl already knew me and knew I loved her.

In my heart, I felt like I was doing this right and it was making up for the hurt that came from never knowing my dad. Morgan was born on May 7 1998 at 10pm. She had thick black hair, (that would later turn to her mommy's blonde) and huge deep blue eyes and was just a tiny little angel. She never cried even once except a singular "waah" when they pricked her heel to do a PK test. Other than that, she was quiet and slept on her mommy's tummy almost instantly. From the very first moment, I could not get enough. I held her for hours in the hospital. It was a very tough delivery for Holly and she had been quite near death. So she didn't mind my taking extra time with Morgan and letting her rest.

Morgan was everything to me. When she was four she did a beautiful little wall hanging for me in Pre School for father's day. The teacher asked the class some questions about their dads and each child answered from their hearts.

The teachers wrote down the child's exact answer no matter how silly. Some of the questions appear here, followed by Morgan's answers in italic:

My dad is _____ year old. *Her answer...7.*

(This is old when you are four!)

My dad is _____ feet tall. *Her answer...10*

My dad weighs about _____ pounds. *446*

My dad likes to watch____. *Race cars and News*

I like it when my dad_____. *Chops food*

(I am a gourmet cook and Morgan has always

been fascinated to watch me working in the

Kitchen)

The most important answer she gave was to this

question...

My daddy always tells me_____ *He loves me.*

I could not hide my tears when I read that. I had spent a lifetime never once hearing a dad tell me he loved me, and here was my four year old daughter telling her teacher that the first thing she thinks of when she thinks of what daddy always tells her is that he loves her. I was doing it right! I was a dad and a good one. Having no example of unconditional love, I sometimes found myself determining to outdo myself when it came to Morgan and thereby maintain my perfect dad status…and keep her love.

Fortunately, being a good dad has produced a terrific kid who does not need new performances from me. Morgan is all I could ask for and then some and she feels the same way about me. I have released that need to God and it's a good thing. The natural progression of things is for her to have less interest in hanging out with dad as years go by. If my self worth is still determined by her love for me, I am doomed to sadness and depression as that progression takes place. I was also allowing myself to be determined as a man by how others saw me as a father as well. The common complement I receive over the years has been "you are a wonderful father." I needed to hear that too. In fact, I remember calling my father three days after Morgan was born. I was thinking, *"Maybe now he'll want a relationship…if not for me then for his grand daughter. Maybe now he will see something good in me because I am a dad. Maybe now he'll want to come around"* What I was really saying inside, but was afraid to say aloud, was *maybe now he would love me.* But that didn't happen either. The greatest moment of my life and I wanted to share it with him and it didn't work.

Holly and I married on Valentines Day 1997 with an eye on me continuing my pursuit of med school. I was only 2 semesters short of my bachelors so that was a given, as we thought, and I would just work until I was accepted. In September, all those plans changed. Even though we had been practicing birth control like religion and even though Holly had been ill for a good portion of the month, we found out we were expecting a baby. For about 8 hours, we were afraid, and then we were ecstatic. I was finally going to be a dad. I was beside my self with joy. To this day it was still one of the greatest moments of my life, finding out we were having a baby. Every great day since then has involved my daughter as well.

One by-product of this, however, was that we made the decision that I would no longer pursue medical school. Holly is not a person who sees the value of sacrificing the present for the future. For us to live in an apartment with a baby was not acceptable, she made that clear. So I gave up on my plans for med school. But I wouldn't trade my daughter for anything...including an M.D. I have a college education and two years worth of memories of working with the finest pediatric orthopedist on earth, and gaining his respect. That was worth more than I can say. But it did put added pressure on my marriage to succeed.

Now that I was not going to be known as a pediatric orthopedist, whatever I did do for a living was going to be plan B. And it wasn't going to be as fulfilling or as important as seeing my vision for my life come true. No, I was going to be known as Craig Daliessio, the husband and father who happened to be a mortgage banker. Therefore, the husband and father thing had to succeed. When it didn't…when my marriage failed, it was just another on a list of dreams that never came true for me. I was not a pro hockey player, I wasn't a doctor, I would never be a beloved son, and now I wasn't a husband in a successful marriage. I added my wife to the list of people who were supposed to love me for my lifetime, just the way I was, and chose not to. My marriage felt like my last chance to validate myself as a man and now it was gone too.

I think that was why I clung so tightly to it and it hurt so much to lose. I needed to get alone with God and let Him define me. I needed to see myself as His beloved child, treasured and desired, but I reacted to God as if He was my own father. I assumed His rejection of me and in turn began to reject Him. Instead of being defined as a man of God and as a child of His, I wrapped myself in the cloak of yet another rejection, this one more devious and painful than all the others combined, and I turned it all inward.

I saw myself as failing yet again, and that failure defining me and devaluing me even further. I was so ashamed, so beaten and so broken, and because of my situation, so isolated. I was ripe for picking when the devil began to attack my heart and soul. He didn't miss his chance. Many, many times I would be in church, maybe standing and singing, and I would glance to my right and imagine Holly and Morgan being there. And just as quickly I would hear him whispering in my ear *"but she's not here is she? You're still alone in church you loser! The picture doesn't look so good now does it, you loser? How could God love you when you failed this badly?"* I took his bait hook line and sinker and lost years of time I could have been worshipping God, spending it instead, running from Him, convinced He was more disappointed in me than I was myself. Of all the pain divorce has forced upon me, my time away from Morgan has wounded the deepest.

The little pre-school Father's day project I mentioned at the start of this chapter is inspired artwork for me. It explains our time together perfectly…it is also the inspiration for the title of this book, and I quoted it in the opening. It is a snapshot of what life is like when you love your child and yet you can't be with her every day. It tells the tale of tears that never completely dry, and sadness that never truly ends. It's a peek through the knothole in the fence around a man's heart and the pain he feels when he loses all that matters and tries to deal with the aftermath. My fatherhood is always a little unsettled, always incomplete. The time we spend together is punctuated by the uneasy feeling that lurking in the shadows is the knowledge that the clock is running and I won't see her for more than a few days at a time.

I am always daddy but I am not always there. And that never stops hurting. I only have so many days and so much time before she is grown and gone on to the adult world. Divorce has cut into that precious commodity with the ferocity of a lion. I am aware of the value of every single second. I plan every weekend for days before, to make sure we create memories and share moments. I am in a rush to cram all I can into the tiny window of opportunity afforded me every other weekend. It isn't fair. It isn't right...and nobody notices.

Chapter 10

*How do you miss
what you've never had?*

During this period after Morgan was born…

… and then when Holly began to verbalize her desire to divorce me and then she finally left, and especially during the time after our divorce, I would often think of my father. I thought about him long before that, but during that period, it grew intense. It was such a cobbled experience, finding out about him when I was 21. Not approaching him for 6 years while I digested it all. Finally contacting him only to be rejected repeatedly. I remember one time especially, I had returned to college at age 30 to finish my degree, two years before I met Holly. I was attending Liberty University and had tried out for the hockey team. Hockey was my passion and I dreamed of playing for L.U. The night the final cuts were announced we met in a classroom on campus. Our captain, Cory Walyuchow announced the final roster and I was included. I was beyond ecstatic. They handed us our jerseys and we had a brief meeting and then went home. I walked in the door of my apartment and, like a little boy; I slipped on my jersey and stood in front of a mirror. I had done it…I was a college hockey player.

I actually had tears in my eyes. This was about 10 years overdue and I relished the moment. Then, seemingly from nowhere, I got the notion to call my father. I actually reached for the phone and in that same instant I snapped back into reality. I couldn't call my dad. We had never spoken. My father was a college graduate himself. At that time, he had his Masters and was working on a PhD. He taught school his entire professional life and was well loved and respected by his students. He had also been a college football player, and played tight end. Something inside me needed my dad to know I was in college too, and I was also an athlete, but I had to stifle that notion instantly. The next day I called Bob and Cathy and celebrated the news with them.

There were other times after that when I needed my dad. When the first signs of marital failure began to show. The first cracks in the wall. I wanted to call him, maybe go get a bite to eat and just talk about what was going on. It was, in my mind, what fathers and sons did together when they progressed to an adult peer relationship. But I never could and so I sailed the uncharted waters of marriage and hit the rocks over and over. I really needed my dad and he wasn't there, and it was by choice. I made contact finally when we moved to Nashville. A few months before Morgan was born I called him. He seemed busy and a little irritated that I'd called. He said he would call me back but he never did. I lost track of it because of all that was happening with Morgan's arrival. When she was born, I called him again to inform him that he had a grandaughter. Maybe this would be the icebreaker at last, I thought, but he just wasn't interested in developing a relationship, and that was that. I went through three years of a very volatile, strained marriage without the advice of the man who might have helped keep me going.

I still idolized him. My dad is a war hero, twice

decorated in Vietnam. He did a second tour just so he could get college money. He is the 13th of 15 children born to immigrant parents and the first to attend college. He now has a PhD in education and is a retired teacher. He was beloved by his students. He married and raised two wonderful children who are successful in their own right. Both my brother and my sister point to their dad as the finest man they've known. He was a dad for them, much as I am to Morgan and they show it in their lives by the success and stability it lends. I met almost all of my cousins and aunts and uncles and I have been accepted with open arms into the fold. They love Morgan, and me and we love them in return.

To hear me talk, you would think I grew up with my dad. I brag about his accomplishments and I am very proud of all he has done. Never once did bitterness or anger creep in. I don't even know if that's healthy. I have wondered if I was so accepting of his rejection that I didn't even see myself as having been wronged or slighted…or even rejected. I think I wore that particular mantle so well that his rejection didn't even seem wrong somehow. But I know I missed him terribly, although I had never even known him. Now I found myself divorced and alone and there were about a million times when I needed to pick up the phone and hear my dad tell me I was going to be alright; but I couldn't.

There are men out there whose fathers passed away who feel that way as well, in my defense, it's not quite the same. When your dad dies, you can process it as the natural course of things. Even if they die young, it wasn't on purpose. However, when your dad rejects you out of hand, that is a difficult thing to make any sense of. Throw in the fact that my father is essentially larger than life and heroic and his rejection seems to somehow be logical. Deep down inside I felt like if *he* rejected me there must be something to it. (Holly would remind me of this thought during our worst battles, twisting that knife as often as she could) I needed to succeed in my marriage to maybe show him I was not a loser and it would be okay for him to accept me. Maybe somehow I was an embarrassment to him and if I could establish myself in life, he would come around to loving me.

Performance again, I know, but that was so deeply engrained in me that I never saw the tragic nature of that thinking until much later…too late in fact. I consciously molded myself into the kind of dad he was. I read my sisters biography when she was competing in the Miss Philadelphia contest in 2000. She stated that her dad was her hero and she was proud of him for all he had overcome and he was her role model and best friend. I poured myself into becoming that for Morgan. To be honest…it was easy. I adored her and no matter what I gave her, she gave me back more in love and happiness.

Being a great dad came naturally to me, and I know that I have my father to thank for that. While I don't know much about him personally, I do know that I am a lot like him in ways that matter. I am a wonderful father and I love learning. I love learning about anything at all.

When I was a kid, I read as if I was being paid by the page. My mother used to tease me because I read the cereal boxes at breakfast. My daughter is like that too. In kindergarten, she was reading at a sixth grade level. By third grade, she was reading her mom's college level nursing books and comprehending most of it. She is a gifted and wonderful child, cut from the same cloth as her daddy and her grandfather. I missed my father terribly in those days, and my divorce made me feel even more rejected by him. These were times when I needed my dad and even this tragedy wouldn't bring him out of the woodwork and into my life. I couldn't earn his love with success and I couldn't gain his pity in my failure.

There is a reason I relate this story of my father in this work, and it is not to decry him. It is because I was guilty of doing something so many of us do. As much as I knew better, I began to transfer the lack of relationship with my dad, onto God. God referred to Himself throughout scripture as my Father. I began to see Him as I saw my father...rejecting, untouched by my grief, superior, distant. In times that normally drove men to their knees, I resolved to remain standing. I could not pray. I was so sure that God was uninvolved in the entire process that I saw it as a useless exercise. God saved me; the rest was up to me. I missed the similarity completely...my father brought me into this world...the rest was up to me. I attributed this to God and the distance between Him and me grew and grew. He was not doing the moving, but I was moving enough for both of us. I began to transfer the anger I should have been feeling towards my father onto God. I would not let myself say a harsh word about my dad, but I screamed them at God in the night. I wouldn't ever attach any anger to his rejection of me and his abdication of his fatherhood and status as grandfather, but I was certain that God had abandoned me and I was furious with Him. I accepted this false rejection just as I had all the others…without a question. I was mad about it, but I never once questioned whether it was true. I never once looked into scripture, saw His promises to be a loving Father, and countered my own thoughts with them. When I read those verses in my darkest hours I was totally convinced they were for everyone else in the world except me. For whatever reason, I was the lone exception to every promise he had made in His word. God didn't care at all about what was happening to me and I was actually accepting of that. Now I didn't have to pursue Him for an answer because He did not intend to give me one. Now I didn't have to ask him to move on my behalf because He was not going to do that for me. Despite His repeated promises in His word, I was resigned to the fact that He did not include me in those promises and I was on my own. See, my father was a perfect dad to the two children he had planned on and wanted, but I was rejected completely with no rights of sonship or familial interaction. Whatever love he had reserved in his father's heart was spent on my brother and sister. So naturally, I could see God doing this to me as well. Despite His promises, and despite what I knew of His character, it seemed very understandable that He was capable of rejecting me over others. After all, my own father had. It gave me freedom to blame Him and hate Him. He rejected me, or so I thought, so I would reject Him. My anger seethed and I was buried in misery and turned it all toward God. My skewed vision of fatherhood actually made me look at Him as if he was the same father who had been rejecting me. Until I finally *only* saw myself as being rejected by Him and my divorce was further proof. Instead of telling my dad *"You could have called…you could have given me advice…"* I said those things to God. *"You could have stopped her! You could have done something to stop this!"* I would alternately lash out at Him and ignore Him completely. He became the focal point for my response to my fathers' rejection, my stepfathers' neglect and oppression, and the countless other broken promises the world had laid at my door. Everyone, except my daughter, who was ever supposed to love me unconditionally, had decided to quit. I resigned myself to that and it snowballed into a self-fulfilling prophecy.

Now my marriage, the one thing I had placed all my hope for success and definition in, had failed as well. It was more than I could bear. In addition, through all of this, deep in my heart, was a cry for my dad. I missed what I dreamed I might have had. Maybe if he had been a part of my life I would had graduated college on time instead of 28 years late. Maybe I would have gone to med school before I ever even met Holly. Maybe we would have had a different life together if I had been included in his family from the start. Maybe I would have gotten through the difficulties in marriage if I had him to lean on. Maybe now I would be happy if he had only been a part of my life. His total absence left me a lot of room to romanticize about it. The "what might have been view" was so attractive. It was easy to slip into a picture of what life might have been like with a great dad to guide me into adulthood and help me navigate the choppy waters of marriage. However, I didn't have any of that and when I began to reap from that seed; I blamed the only Father who was still around...God.

He didn't deserve it and none of it was true, but I dished it out anyway. All the anger, all the disappointment, all the hurt and pain. I ceased praying completely, except prayers with Morgan. Praise and worship at my church became a battle to control my pain and rage. Anything that would usher me into His presence was avoided with increasing effort. I would leave the sanctuary during praise time, or stand there with an angry scowl. I quit going to the mid week bible study I belonged to. I missed church for any small reason. This became all God's fault and I was distancing myself from Him...so I thought anyway. I couldn't lash out at my dad. I couldn't tell him what his rejection of me was doing to me and how much it hurt. I couldn't tell him he was wrong and I did need him and my island was barren, desolate, and lonely. I couldn't hear his voice. I couldn't see his face shine on me. I never knew what he looked like when he smiled. He refused to be approached and I couldn't even vent my anger about *that* to him.

So I wrapped it all in a nice ball and laid it on God instead. He became all of those hurts and all of those rejections and all of that pain. I turned it all against Him and lashed out with all the fury of a hurricane. He was, after all, the only father figure still around. My adopted dad, Bob, was 900 miles away and with all that they had endured losing their daughter, I never wanted to trouble them with my problems. No, I was alone here in Tennessee with no father around except God and He was going to have to take what I was dishing out. It bordered on hatred and it seemed bottomless. I lashed out relentlessly; *"Once again I was abandoned and alone and You saw this coming! You could have stepped in and saved my marriage, You could have done something! You could have shown up when we called You, You could have run interference for me while I was learning the ropes in a new career. You could have miraculously supported us in the lean times. But You never did anything! You hid yourself and remained far away and abandoned me to my pain and now I have lost the only things I loved. And You never even noticed!"* It doesn't take a rocket scientist to see where these outrageous painful statements came from, but in my darkness, I never put the two together. I was determined to blame God for all of this and I saw Him as a rejecter, just like my dad. Having defined myself by the success of my marriage and seeing that fail, I was convinced that God was rejecting me like everyone else and I no longer had time for it. To make matters worse, the one area I had left, fatherhood, was now being limited. When you are divorced you don't have unlimited access to your child anymore. So here I was, the only positive defining element of my life was my fatherhood, and I was only performing my daddy role once a week and every other weekend. The times in between were filled with loneliness beyond measure and angry, bitter, pain. I felt like I wore a scarlet letter somehow. I felt like the biggest loser on the planet and everyone knew it. I felt rejected and isolated from the world. I had once painted a picture of my life where I was an athlete and I liked it. When it didn't happen, I accepted it without any problem. Then I once imagined myself maybe coaching hockey for a living and even went so far as to send out a few resumes but decided to return to college instead. Again, no problem accepting that change of fate. Next came my pursuit of a medical career. That was moving along well and I was excited to finally have found something that I had real passion about and interest in. That too, had to be laid at the feet of the changes life throws at you. I swallowed a little harder at that one, but I accepted that I got the better part of the deal when I saw Morgan for the first time.

Now I was again finding myself being redefined by life. And this time I protested. I hated the newest version of the snapshot of my life. Being a dad was all I had left to cling to and now even that was being limited and doled out to me like daily rations. I only felt like a dad when I had Morgan, so what did that make me in between visits? Again, my value as a man was contained within the bounds of my life as a dad. It seemed like this was the only thing left that I did really well. I desperately needed my fatherhood to be intact and now even that was restricted. This only added to the reasons why this divorce was hurting me so very much. As a final illustration of this chapter, let me give you an analogy from my past. I've had many friends ask me what it did to me inside when I found out at 21, the truth about my father. Living in the computer age as we do, I can best describe it like this. Imagine using your computer at home or work and in the middle of a very intricate, detailed process, you reached in and yanked out the hard drive, and installed another one with a totally different operating system. For the sake of explanation let's say you swapped a PC for a MAC, midstream. (I know, computer geeks, it can't be done, but humor me here) Every calculation, every computation, all your stored files, all the memory on your memory cards, everything would be corrupted and altered. Nothing would work properly and your computer would be a mess. Even if you could get it to function, little about the computer would be the same. The keyboard characters would probably not be what they appear to be on the board. The files would not contain what they say on the directory, etc. Nothing would function as it had before. In human terms, truth would now be a lie. Everything I thought I knew about myself was now brought into question and there was an entire new history and genealogy thrown into my mix. Nothing worked the way it used to. Divorce was just like that for me. The frame of reference for my life had been

"I am a husband and a father, everything I do, every decision I make is made in light of that truth." Now that wasn't true anymore. Take away my marriage and there wasn't anything left. As far as I was concerned, without my marriage I was nothing, and that made it hurt even more.

I need to make one very important point here at the end of a very revealing chapter. I love my dad. I have accepted that I will likely never have any sort of relationship with him at all. I will never understand his reticence towards the situation. I will likely carry some sort of hurt from this for the rest of my life. However, in all that I have chosen forgiveness and decided to let it go. In fact, I had considered eliminating this chapter altogether, but it is necessary from one very important perspective, and that is this; many men decide that the pain of maintaining a relationship with their kids, post-divorce, is too much and they give up. I am certain this is what happened to my father. While he and my mother never married, I do know they talked about it and I know what kind of man he is. It was not easy for him to realize that a marriage would have only served to make a bad situation worse. Knowing what I know of his heart, I think he had to make a conscious decision to block out any feelings he had for me and any fatherhood urges just to survive.

I am not excusing this decision or endorsing this path. I am telling this portion of my story because I want dads to understand the consequences of choosing to not be there. I want you to realize the kind of hole you will leave in the heart of your kids if you vanish, either all at once or over time. I want you to know that even a fractured, limited relationship where you see each other every few days is still a relationship. It still feels like you have a dad. You still connect. You can fill in the empty spaces with phone calls and now with the technology of Skype and text messaging you can at least communicate daily. Nothing replaces a hug or physical touch but connection can be maintained.

I also know how hard this is. It hurts. It hurts to talk to your kids on the phone like a prisoner at visitation day. It hurts to keep your heart pliable and vulnerable instead of just walking away and turning hard and cold in order to survive. But from the perspective of a kid who grew up that way let me tell you that it does a lifetime of damage. There are stolen moments that I will never know. Things I wanted to share with my dad that I never will be able to. I related my story not to shame my father…I never even mentioned him by name here…but to explain the hurt so that dads who read this will make the choice to tough it out, suck it up, and be the dad they were called to be. Remember men…you are the daddy. Not because you are married to the mommy, but because have of the DNA that makes up that wonderful blessing of a child comes from you, and not a soul on this planet could have contributed with the same result. Your child is distinct from all others because of the distinct parents God used to create him. You are the daddy because God ordained it that way. You never lose that right…but you can choose to give it up.

Never make that decision.

Chapter 11

*"Who told you
I said that?"
---God*

If we were all honest,

…we would admit that most of us have a less than factual image of God. Some of us see Him as a fire-breathing monster who wants nothing more than to punish us for our wrongs and hurt us even more than our sins hurt us themselves. Some of us see Him as the smiling garden gnome of the prosperity / positive thinking religions that preach that "Every day should be Friday" and "God wants you rich and perfectly healthy" and "God's blessings are always financial and if you aren't rich and happy you don't know God!" Some folks know only the dusty, silent, stone-faced God of liturgy and orthodoxy and He has never become a living, breathing, loving being in their lives. Some cling to theology and knowledge at the sacrifice of intimacy with their Creator. Some dance around like blithering idiots and know only emotional, shallow responses to a mystical God. Ask 100 Christians from various walks of life and you might get 100 different definitions of who and what God is.

Along with this hodge-podge of images of Him, is the hodge-podge of teachings about what He feels and thinks about any given topic. Some churches teach that He is okay with various sins while other churches teach that He hates certain things more than others. It seems that one of the universally held beliefs among almost every church and every denomination and most Christian people is that "God hates divorcees. Now the verse actually says "God hates divorce" (Malachi 2:16) but for so many years now...all of my life and even well before...the pulpits in most mainstream denominations have preached about divorce not from a sympathetic position, but from a spirit of condemnation. I agree with Scripture on this and every other social issue...divorce is not God's way. However, the ostracizing of divorcees is also not His way.

The selection of this particular sin as more evil than say alcoholism or pornography or gambling...that was wrong. I understand how it happened. Divorce is—on the surface at least—seemingly easy to prevent. You simply say "No." You simply refuse to get a divorce. You dig in and stand on the biblical principles of marriage and you endure and God will bless. However, this mindset was developed long before the days of "No-Fault Divorce." For those unclear as to what that means, let me explain. In the U.S. right now, every state is a "no-fault" state. What this means, in a nutshell, is that you don't actually need a real reason to get divorced anymore. You simply have to want to get divorced. It's no longer a covenant in the eyes of the court, it's a contract, and by law, every state recognizes this contract has an out-clause. If you want out, you can get out. Most of the time this falls under the description of "irreconcilable differences." The only thing really debated is how much this out-clause will cost each party. If there is adultery or abuse involved, the offending party will likely pay a higher price, in the form of limits on child visitation and monetary compensation. If the man cheated or abused he will pay higher alimony. If the women cheated or abused and she was not the main breadwinner, she will get less. But no judges in the U.S. will ever just sit back, look at the file and say "No…you guys need to work this out. There isn't enough here to dissolve a marriage." It used to be that way, but no-fault laws ended that. The name is what it implies… "It's nobody's fault…we're just getting divorced"

I am not here to debate the right or wrong with this law. But it bares explanation because in the eyes of most churches, *someone has to be blamed.* They can't accept that perhaps one party didn't want this but was powerless to stop it. Therefore, they typically view divorcees as someone to be blamed. If you are a man in a divorce, you feel the accusations without ever hearing them. "He must have cheated. He must have been abusive. He must have gambled away the mortgage. I bet he drinks." And on it goes.

The church somehow cannot grasp that its members might simply not want to be married to their spouse anymore. Yes, there were problems but none that rose to scriptural reasons for divorce. The church taught, since its inception, that you stay in a marriage because it is a covenant between two people and God and that covenant should never be broken except for within very specific guidelines. You practice forgiveness and restoration. You respond as Christ did. You stay together.

This is all well and good if the laws of the land cooperate. And there was a time when they did. Now we live in a disposable marriage society and the same laws apply to Christians as well as non-believers. The problem is changing the attitude of the Church. And I don't mean changing the scriptural position on divorce. Rather, realizing that the divorce laws are written with Free Will in mind. That now, a godly man or woman no longer has the option of refusing to grant their unhappy spouse a divorce and digging in their heels and waiting for a miracle. The church needs to understand that divorce is now about as easy as breaking a contract to buy a house. There is money involved as penalty for not completing the deal, but you can get out of it if you wish, for no other reason than you wish to get out of it.

The Church is still treating divorcees like second-class citizens. They still place restrictions one how a divorcee can serve. They still refuse some of us ministry opportunities and they still see us as failures. They subconsciously think we just "quit" on our marriage, didn't have enough faith that God would change our spouse, or didn't really want to make it work in the first place. This is unfair and it creates a huge distance between the wounded divorcees and the fellowship of Saints that we so desperately need to be a part of in such a horrible time.

Then too, it creates a view of God that drives us further away from Him instead of drawing us closer. It is obvious to anyone who has a shred of knowledge about the God of scripture, that my view of Him had become twisted. I was going to use the word skewed, but skewed wouldn't nearly cover it. It was Picasso-esque. The God of my world made Scrooge look like St. Ignacious. But how did He go from the smiling God of my Sunday school flannel graphs to this angry, hateful, unconcerned, capricious, conditionally loving, lightning bolt thrower? How could a God be so motivated by love that He sent His son to die a horrible death to secure my soul, and then ignore me after that? Where did that come from and who taught it to me? The answer is twofold.

First and foremost, that example was set out in my home growing up. My mother and stepfather were both the products of dysfunction. They had huge gaping holes in their own hearts that needed filling. They never put that active search for contentment on hold while raising a family. In fact, having children got in the way of their relentless pursuit of what would make them happy. Instead of pouring themselves into their children, we were regarded as a great inconvenience. They were a couple with four kids, who preferred to be left alone. This made for a lonely upbringing. By the time I was seven years old, I was playing little league and the coaches became my surrogates. While I screamed inside for someone at home to notice me, I at least had someone *outside* the house that did. If anything good came about from the disconnect I felt toward my stepfather, it was that it made it okay for me to seek father figures elsewhere. Part of me longed for his approval and bond, the other part of me felt that his treatment of me gave me license to replace him with coaches, and other boys' dads. In my house, performance was not everything, it was the only thing. My mother was quite literally a different person hour to hour. If she was morose, it fell on my shoulders to make her laugh. So I grew up learning to perform for love and carried that into my marriage. I never rested in it, but always sought further reassurance.

Again, sports probably saved my life because at least there I had coaches giving me approval and I had become a favorite with the other boy's parents. I was always good for a joke and I extended the performance thing to parents outside my home. I found the attention I craved and felt like I had family. I hated when baseball season ended. It would be all winter long before I could see those families again and feel some of what I was missing. My stepfather was never a part of anything I did. Every great achievement on the field, everything I did in the classroom, every award. He was nowhere to be found, and eventually I stopped looking. He was cold, unapproachable, and distant. That was what I thought of when I thought of a dad. So perhaps it was only natural that as I grew up and tried to perceive God as a Father, I could only draw on two possible examples of fatherhood. One man who didn't want me even though I was his and one man who pretended like I was his and didn't want me. Either way I felt I was unwanted and isolated by whatever father figure I had at home, and inside my heart

I drew on that as the compass point on which my vision of God the Father would swing.

The other aspect to this two-headed snake that was my perception of God was the religious upbringing I had as a child. My mother had accepted Christ in 1973, after a small earthquake scared her in the middle of the night. The next day she had called out to God and that Sunday we began attending a church in a small subdivision about five miles from our house. It was, at that time, a "community church" meaning they were not particularly aligned with any denomination, although they were essentially Baptist by doctrine. It was a friendly, warm, welcoming place and the pastor was a great man of tremendous vision and character. They had a big Sunday school program with buses that would pick you up each Sunday if you didn't have a ride. The teachers were friendly and the people were gracious. They had special music in the main services and they were very talented singers. I enjoyed those early years at that church very much. Of course longing for a father figure, I instantly attached myself to the male Sunday school teachers I had. One man in particular was Bill Bell. He was a short man with a ton of energy, a kind smile, and a warm drawl to his voice. He was from Oklahoma and was living in Delaware, working at the Chrysler plant while he finished his degree. He had three kids around my age. He became my friend and my favorite teacher.

Within weeks, I was going with him on Saturday mornings to visit the other kids on our bus route. I was even reading the bible with these kids and praying with them. At 8 years old, I was quite a hit with the adults because of my devotion to the cause. I was serious about my desire for God, but it didn't hurt that it got me some attention from some wonderful male role models. Looking back, between my coaches and the men I aligned myself with to replace my missing father, I was very blessed that none of them were predatory. As much as I needed their approval and as much time as I spent in their presence I could have very easily been victimized.

In a way, I was, but not in the fashion you would suspect. Around 1979 or 1980, a traveling evangelist came to our church. He had been coming there every year since 1975 and preaching about end time prophecy and such. He was interesting and dramatic in his presentation, but until 1979, he had not been dangerous. I don't know what changed in his life to alter the content of his weeklong revivals but change he did. He began to preach sermons increasingly engulfed in the chains of legalism. He preached about a God who grew angrier and angrier and meaner and meaner, one sermon was an entire hour about the evils of women wearing pants. The sermon was a rail against women who wore anything that pertained to men but particularly pants, and it culminated with his mind-boggling recitation of a story he alleged took place somewhere in Arkansas. He swore this was true and told it with great gusto. A woman in this church he was preaching at was particularly fidgety and obviously disturbed and agitated by his sermon about women wearing pants. She twisted and rolled her eyes and as soon as the sermon ended, she raced for the door before he could even have one of his famous 20-minute altar calls. On her way out, he couldn't help but notice she wore pants. Later that week the pastor relayed to him that he had received a scathing note from the woman concerning the visiting evangelists' meddling in her dress code and her private affairs. She was angry and considering leaving the church and she would never even once think about not wearing pants. This evangelist spent a few minutes painting a picture based on conjecture, of why this woman really wanted to wear pants. She was a rebellious wife whose husband didn't keep her in line. She was out of order based on Paul's teachings about a woman's place under her husband in God's hierarchy. She was a trollop, who wanted to show her butt to the world, and it was all about sex and she was a Jezebel. Then he finished the story with the sort of story that looking back, should have earned him an Oscar...and a ticket out of that church on a rail.

With a gleam in his eye and the kind of wanderlust that causes a man to drool while he speaks, he told us of returning to this same church one year later for another weeklong revival. The pastor greeted him at the airport and as they were driving to his hotel room, the pastor said, "Brother Dunn...we have to stop by the hospital, there is someone we need to visit there." So they go to the hospital and arrive in a room in the oncology department. And there lying in a bed is the woman who stormed out of his anti-pants sermon one year earlier. She had no legs from the knees down, both taken dramatically by cancer. And according to this charlatan's retelling, she *"reached up...grabbed my lapels...and through tears she sobbed these words...preacher...keep preaching the sermon about women wearing pants! I've got no legs now preacher! God took my legs because I wore pants!"* And the church ate that stuff up like candy.

He preached more sermons like that in his revival meetings that year, and before he was done, he had damaged our view of God and His love and Grace so profoundly, that the church was never again the same. The pastor was a man who cared deeply about his people and I think he fell for this graceless view because he saw it as a way to eliminate temptation. (In the years since, this church has become somewhat more centrist, but sadly, many other churches remain slaves to legalism). That breaks my heart to this day because looking back now as an adult, I know he loved his people very much. But his love was not (at the time) wrapped in the belief that God was the better Father and would take care of His children in *His* way.

His love for us became the source for a sort of paranoia about codes of conduct and micro legalism. We out-legislated the Catholics when it came to rules and regulations and it drove people into a performance based belief system that ruined an entire generation. Hellfire and brimstone was the order of the day. Dads were described as authoritarian punishers and if you were a "godly man," you ruled your house with an iron fist and your children feared you. You threw out the TV and banished any form of music except that which the pastor defined as right. As he was a much older man, our tastes in music never really matched but I pushed myself to try to like what he defined as acceptable. More performance based living. We were constantly surrounded by sayings like "I'm just a sinner saved by grace" and lyrics to songs that portrayed the saved as the single most undeserving bunch of worthless dung heaps in existence.

And the really bad news was that God still saw us in that way. We were all lucky to just be alive and going to heaven. Other than that singular act of redemption, God was angry with us and we had better been on our best behavior for the rest of our lives because God was keeping that Bema seat thing in His back pocket just in case we screwed up. Just when we thought we were safe and had made it to heaven, He was going to judge our works after all…even though we were saved by grace through faith…and brother, going to hell had nothing on barely getting into heaven. God was going to be angry with us for eternity if we didn't read twice as much bible as we watched TV and if we parted our hair in the middle. It was actually not restricted to just this one church. It was the general mood of independent Baptist churches around this time.

The pulpits were stuffed with obese evangelists who ran their homes like tyrants, abused their kids with legalism, suppressed the dreams and hopes of their wives, and oppressed their households with heavy-handed gracelessness. All the while in the churches, in their revival meetings, they went on hour-long rants about the evils of cigarettes and the latest Imperials album. God had killed Elvis because he had wandered away from his walk with Christ. God cut off the legs of rebellious women and caused car accidents to happen to wicked teenagers who stayed out past 9PM.

God was famous around this time for "putting you on the shelf" which was a code word for killing you, if you fell away from Him in any way. God disapproved of Billy Grahams' haircut and God didn't believe that famous athletes could really change and give their hearts to Jesus. God hated abortion, but God hated Catholics even more, and so when Jerry Falwell invited the Archbishop of the Richmond Diocese to speak at Liberty University, along with other opponents of abortion, our pastors railed on him for it. God was angry, capricious, mean, hateful, graceless, loveless, and He really had a grudge against us for making Calvary necessary in the first place.

This is the God who also *hated divorce*, and so when I found myself divorced I simply could not forgive myself. I felt like I had failed God so terribly and He had no use for me whatsoever now. I was disqualified from any sort of service and relegated to second-class citizen status. I had come so far from the days when I saw God in this fashion and had made giant strides escaping that legalism but somehow, getting a divorce took me back to that belief system. Divorce peeled off a giant layer of my onion and under the surface, this angry, graceless system of religion had been lurking. To a lesser degree no doubt, but I still slipped into a belief that God was angry with me, disappointed in me, and therefore He was not going to intervene in any way, neither to help restore my marriage, nor to help bring me comfort. I had extended His grace too far and I was on my own. In fact I was lucky He didn't just kill me...I mean put me on the shelf.

Chapter 12

...Where morning dawns

and evening fades...

Given this twisted view of God…

… that had been drilled into my head from early childhood, it's no wonder that I fell into a belief that God was angry and that all He would do was reject me. With that sort of stored information, how could I really come to any other conclusion? Nevertheless, God was not going to let me go that easily and I believe He had enough of people sullying His reputation as a Father.

In 1993, I discovered a wonderful book entitled "The Ragamuffin Gospel." The author was Brennan Manning and he would instantly become my favorite Christian writer of all time. He had a grasp on communicating grace to those wounded by legalism and I lapped it up. When David cries in Psalm 42 "As the deer pants for streams of water, so my soul pants for you, oh God," I believe he was describing the longing of the inner man for the grace of a loving God. When you finally find it, it is truly like a deer that longs to find a stream and finally does. The hunters had been pursuing for years and years and I was so very weary of being on the run. My flight had taken place in a barren land and even if I had found water, I couldn't stop to drink.

Occasionally I found an old stagnant pool full of the same stale, lifeless poison. I could no longer hold my nose and drink it down. This was the very stuff I was running from. Besides all that, the hunters would not relent. Into that scene, in November of 1993 came a perfect storm of God's grace. Earlier that fall I had begun renting an apartment from Bob and Cathy and they had slowly begun to include me in their wonderful family. The day before Thanksgiving, 1993 I purchased the book I just mentioned, *The Ragamuffin Gospel*, and at 6PM that night began reading it. I could not put it down. I devoured Brennan's illustrations of grace and stories of mercy and a loving God. I wept, and in the weeping layer upon layer of walls began to crumble.

I saw for the first time that God was motivated by love...and ONLY by love. Sin and punishment were our doing. His motivation was never anger and rage. People did not go to hell because He sent them there with a smirk. They walked in under their own power with a weeping God in their rear view mirror. He did everything He could to stop that and He paid an ultimate price to make it avoidable. There was only one way to avoid eternal damnation and only He could provide it. And when everything in the world would have pointed to just letting us all die in our miserable state and go to hell as an entire species, God chose to do what made no sense to anyone but Him. He willingly chose to let His Son be brutally butchered at our hands, the saved murdering the savior, so that we could have a chance at life eternal.

THAT was Grace! And in the face of that kind of love, how could anyone believe that God cared about the part in my hair or whether my wife wore pants. Did He expect circumspect living? Absolutely, but He was going to accomplish that by drawing me ever closer into His loving Presence with the lure of love and Grace. In that Presence I would just naturally change into *His* perfect vision for me. A vision that was different from His vision for everyone else. We retained our individuality under His Grace. No uniforms, no performance goals, and no stars on God's refrigerator for only the good little boys and girls. Grace was for everyone or it was not, by definition, Grace.

The opportunity was universal, and only our own choice made it individual in its application. I read until midnight, awoke at six the next morning, and finished the book before noon. I wept, laughed, and smiled and after all that, I prayed in freedom for the first time in my life. God loved me…He didn't love me in some manipulative, performance driven fashion because He was eternally needy and had to have me tell Him how great He was. He loved me, not in spite of there being nothing lovable about the human condition; He loved me *because* there was nothing lovable in the human condition. As Manning said, the Great Hound of Heaven had begun His relentless pursuit, and I was to be His prey. He had taken up the chase and had enough of my wandering in the desert of graceless misery. He was corralling me towards His streams of living water and I had thankfully stopped running. As Brennan so often says, "God loves us as we are, not as we ought to be. Because we are never going to be as we ought to be."

That afternoon, I was invited to Bob and Cathy's

house for Thanksgiving dinner. It was the first time I had been at a Thanksgiving table in my life, where there was not screaming, mayhem, and everything but Thanks. There was laughter, joy, happiness, and love. This was what a family was supposed to be and it capped a wonderful 24 hour period of feasting on the grace of God. I walked in that profound revelation for several years. When I met Holly, I was well adjusted to this Grace. I had been attending a new church for three years. A church that taught the truth about the real God. No legalism, no stifling rules, and angry God lurking over my shoulder, waiting for my next slip.

I grew in this revelation and experience first hand what His reckless wonderful love felt like. Somewhere over he next few years' new layers of my onion were torn off revealing some holes in my grace overcoat. When we started having difficulties in our marriage, I began to fall back into my old pattern of trying to fix it myself. That only led to more failure because I was depending on my own frail abilities instead of God. Then the more I failed, the more pressure I put on myself to succeed next time and the cycle continued. Because both of us were Christians, and we were outwardly seeking God for answers, we both just got more bitter and angry when He didn't step in and do what we demanded.

In retrospect, we were seeking Him, but on our terms. We went to Him in prayer, not seeking His guidance and wanting His wisdom, but with a shopping list of demands for our marriage. God does not function that way. In fact, by nature, He cannot. If I could rattle off my list of demands and He would jump out of obligation, He wouldn't actually be God, would He? Of course, this is hindsight. When I was living through it, I only saw it as God failing to act and that morphed into God abandoning me. I only believed He could abandon me because I was raised in a performance based belief system and *that* God certainly could leave me alone in my pain. Jesus comforting words *"Remember I am with you even until the end of all time"* were long forgotten, replaced instead by the fierce silence of an angry God who stood by while I writhed in pain, arms folded across His chest, deep in thought about how next to punish me.

I had essentially slipped back into that graceless, merciless system of lies that I grew up with and it was going to take some serious extrication this time. In retrospect I hadn't reverted, back as much as I had been pared down to reveal another larger and far more sinister layer of this deceit. The God I thought hated and abandoned me, was, in fact, getting ready to walk with me through the deepest, darkest, most painful valley I had ever known. It would be a lonely, desolate, isolating, painful path, but the fruit of that journey would be the removal of the root from which that deceitful view of God sprang. He was going to allow me to be torn asunder and wounded deeply, my hip popped thoroughly from its socket. And when the sun would next rise on the moment of my own Peniel, like Jacob I was going to be walking off toward the Promised Land, limping from my wrestling match with God Himself. Limping but victorious, marked forever as a man who went all 12 rounds with God and by losing to His Grace, I won the greater prize.

In His touch, I was changed forever and from that point on, whenever someone saw my limping gait, he would know I had been with God, and I had wonderful stories to tell about the battle. God was not going to let me live the rest of my life convinced He had abandoned me. The lies I had been told about Him were an insult to Him and He was set on changing my perceptions forever. He had it in His mind to be my Father and He had graciously allowed me to run out of both excuses and room. This was going to hurt, but this was going to change me forever in ways I needed to be changed. I truly believe, looking back, that God allowed, and maybe even ordained, my most vile attacks on Him in my darkest hours.

Those times when I would scream my curses toward heaven and bang my fist at the thoughts of His supposed love for me. I think He had already plumbed the depths of the anguish to which I was going to sink in order to get to the root of my pain and remove this deceit for the last time. The tug of war began between the God Who was there and Who loved me relentlessly, and the god of my upbringing, who gave me His love in small measure doses, only when I read enough chapters of the Bible and burned my rock records. He would have no more of this. He was madly in love with me and He had a plan for finally breaking through to my tortured soul with the relentless hurricane of love He had for me.

In my deepest pain He stayed by my side. When I pushed Him away, he silently let me know He was not going anywhere. Maybe in the beauty of a sunset or in the sweet voice of my daughter telling me she loved me. Sometimes in the words to a wonderful song or on a printed page. Sometimes in silence and sometimes in the joyous exultation around a Christmas dinner table. When I would try to shove Him out the door, He would give me my space but remind me that my space was, in fact His, and He was there even when I didn't want Him to be. In fact, He was, by definition, everywhere or He wasn't God, and so I could not escape Him even if I wanted to. His pursuit was relentless and He had more patience than I ever deserved. He surrounded me with people who He could trust to be His emissaries of grace and mercy. I found myself in the midst of a group of loving, caring children of His who felt called to love me. I found friends where I wasn't looking, and no matter how I tried to ruin those friendships with the self-fulfilling prophecy of my own perceived unlovable-ness, they were motivated by a stronger Spirit and they would not quit. Slowly, gradually, God began to chip away at my hardest shell and tallest wall.

God had begun to bring some new faces into my life.

Instead of people who wished me well from a distance, and told me they were praying for me, they actually prayed for me...right then, right there. Men I barely knew would approach me, put a hand on my shoulder, look me in the eye, and proclaim God's love for me. One such event took place in a local deli. I ran into my friend Brandon and his friend Brian. They sat at my table for a few minutes on the way out. I was in one of my deep funks and my mood was just terrible. Brian had only just met me five minutes prior and he suddenly looked at me and told me "God wants me to tell you he loves you and good things are on their way. He knows you've been hurting and He is with you in your pain."

I resented that notion, made some negative responses and actually at one point reasoned with them both that God had better things to do than concern Himself with my little problems. I railed on them on the outside but inside another little chip flew off the stone walls around my soul. It would be almost four years worth of these little chips before the walls came down but God was working. He was taking the battleground inch by precious inch and this time He was building garrisons to prevent the hard-won ground from ever being relinquished to Satan again. He was tearing out the lies by the root, and laying the groundwork for the massive change He was about to bring. God used an untold number of ways to crystallize the notion of His love for me. They were as varied as a rainbow but there was one common object lesson He was using repeatedly...my daughter.

Over all this time, she was the one example of unconditional love I could see and touch every moment. If I wanted to know what love sounded like I could call her and hear her say *"hi daddy",* or tell me she loved me. Some tiny flame kept flickering even in the coldest corner of my soul because of her. My life was a whirlwind of rage and a hurricane of sorrow and sadness and a thick fog of unkept promises and broken dreams. However, in the quiet breaks in my blustery rage, I could hear the sound of God's inescapable call echoing in the sweet sound of Morgan's voice or in the tenderness of her hugs.

The depth of my sorrow and pain could only be countered by the immeasurable love I have for her. And every once in a while God would whisper in my ear, *"I love you like that…"* Every so often when I was tucking her in and giving her a hug and her tiny frame was engulfed in my arms, God would flash a picture in my soul--a picture of Him holding me in that fashion. Sometimes in this vision, my face might be stained from tears and my fist might be clenched from the pain I was in, but He never noticed any of that. At first God was a hazy figure in the scene, just the almost unimaginable Daddy I longed for, loving me as only a daddy could. But slowly…ever so slowly, he moved from fuzzy to focus. From pan to zoom and it became clear to my aching soul that this was God the Father…God *my* Father…holding me closely to his heart…calming my soul, absorbing the terrible grief I was engulfed in. His words kept echoing in my barren heart… "I heal the brokenhearted and bind up their wounds" " I am a comforter to the comfortless" "I will never leave you and never forsake you and I am with you no matter where you go on this earth…even if you are trying to hide from me".

My daughter taught me more about the love of God than anything else in my world. And it was that example of love that God kept using to hammer home His love for me in a way I could finally grasp and He used that example to help me finally believe that those words of love and compassion and those promises of grace and Fatherhood were meant for me too. The message was simple, if I felt complete and whole when I was loving towards her and holding her in my arms and connecting with her like dads do, than God felt no less for me. He longed for me the way I longed for her. He missed me terribly in between visits, just as I did Morgan. This truth took a while to set in but when it did, it washed over me like waves on a beach. God was relentless in His pursuit and limitless in His bounty when it came to His love for me. The chips in my walls became cracks, and the cracks lead to crumbling. Sometime around the fall of 2006, He began to make His final assault on the fortress of deception that had been hiding the truth from me. Gods' unwavering conquest had gained enough ground that now He could make one final, concentrated drive for the throne of my heart. I spent almost an entire weekend in prayer in October of 2006 and felt God truly tearing down big sections of the battlements. I prayed that He would "sweep out the cobwebs" and "kick open my trap doors and secret passages." I wanted complete truth and openness with Him and he was obliging me.

In the course of the next 18 months, God accelerated His love attack and broke through to my weary soul. He did it by relentlessly hammering home a wonderful truth in my heart. Repeatedly, He reminded me that everywhere throughout scripture were references to His immeasurable love for me. *That* was truth…not the myopic, mean spirited angry god I imagined him to be. Repeatedly he drew me to verses that exposed His wild, passionate love for me, one day in the fall of 2007 it clicked. In the story relayed in another chapter in this book, in fact in the event that motivated this writing, God allowed me the privilege of a look backward, and there I saw it. The unmistakable imprint of His presence beside me through every step, every stumble, every valley, and every mountaintop. He had been there. Some veil had been lifted and I was granted a view through the eyes of the Spirit and I saw Him walking with me through all of it. The disappointing marriage, the divorce, the betrayal, the loneliness, the anger, the fear, the shame, the loss, the weariness. All of it. He showed me how He was bearing it all with me, and that there were lessons to be learned. Then he showed me other men who were wandering in their own darkness looking for a light, certain that God had abandoned them just as I imagined He did me.

One morning in church, as the song leader was leading us in a song and he spoke the simple prayer: *"Lord help us to see ourselves as You see us."* Those words literally leapt into my heart that morning. I offered that same prayer to God and he instantly began answering it. The morning when He ordained this book and my ministry to men like me, he did it by showing me how much He truly loved me and how badly He hurt for me all those years. In addition, he showed me how He was hurting for those others, and how my pain was going to be an instrument of healing to them. The last walls fell and on those stones, He began to build a new fortress of love and acceptance. It has become my home and I am finally safe there with my Father.

But why extend that invitation to others? What is it about my faith that makes me think there is some secret there for handling the pain that divorce brings? Why do I think you need Jesus Christ? Well, I suppose there are many reasons and many ways to answer that question. I have watched the news, as all of us have at one time or another, and seen those stories about some poor guy who has lost his family and decides to end it all and take them with him. I've seen those stories and wondered too. Not how a man could do that but why more men have not. How can a person feel the biting pain of losing the love of his wife and seeing his family disintegrate and *not* become that desperate?

Of course, it's wrong and of course it's an indicator of a deeper problem, and I am not condoning it. But I am amazed at how many guys are hanging on for all they are worth and don't stray over that fine line of insanity or temporary desperation that leads to tragedy. This life hurts. It hurts a lot and without some moral anchor and some grace and healing from somewhere outside of my own soul I don't know how I would have made it. God says He heals the brokenhearted and binds up their wounds. The common bond of Christianity brought other guys into my life to pray and help me. Men have prayed big prayers and loved me in the way only His people do. But it took a long time and a lot of people came and went through my life before, who could have stopped and offered comfort. I have felt His loving touch on my shoulders in my darkest nights. I was never alone even when I thought I wanted to be left alone. I could not make God abandon me and I have never been without His offer of comfort.

I didn't always accept his offering, but He always offered. There is a part of the soul of a man that only His Creator can touch and heal. David says in the Psalms that God "searches out" the inmost parts of a man. That is so necessary if you are going to survive this thing. You need Him because He *made you*. He knows you better than anyone does. He has the answers. He is not angry with you, He does not regret creating you, nor does He regret sending Jesus to die for you. He is not finished with you and He has no plans to put you on some shelf and render you a second class citizen in His plan and His kingdom. He is not the God of the legalists, and you have not crossed some imaginary line in the sand, just because you are divorced. The pain of divorce is punishment enough. God is too busy trying to heal your wounds, to bother with heaping more pain on your shoulders.

Chapter 13

Field of Dreams...

The question should be asked...

...what about now? What has transpired in the 13 years since my divorce? It's strange as I sit here now. I wrote the original version of this book in late 2007 and completed it in 2008. So much has changed since then.

In May 2008, I lost my career in the mortgage industry and began a 4-year ordeal of homelessness. I literally lived in my car from August 2008 until January 2012. During that time I returned to college to complete my Bachelors (changing from Pre-Med to Religion) through Liberty University Online. I wrote a Christmas book called "A Ragamuffin Christmas" which was published last year. I continued writing my blog for divorced dads "Sometimes Daddies Cry" and it became one of the top five most visited divorced dads' blogs on the internet.

However, during all this, I had put my ministry amongst divorced men on hold. I was busy in school, busy trying desperately to find a way out of homelessness, and busy trying to eek out a living as a carpenter. I was trying to maintain a relationship with my daughter, even as I lived in my car. I was determined to remain in her life and active as her daddy even if it meant staying in Nashville and living as I lived.

I would love to tell you that the Church's response to my homelessness was Christ-like and loving but sadly...it was a lot like the general response to my divorce. Ignore it and maybe it will go away. Find reasons to believe it was somehow my fault (as if I were the one who sank the mortgage industry) and tell me to simply go find a job. I was more alone in my homelessness than ever in my life, and this came on the heels of the terrible isolation that my divorce brought about. I was only beginning to get on my feet emotionally and socially and then I lost my entire life. It was a lot to endure and it was more breaking to an already very broken heart.

Nevertheless, through that dreadful experience I pressed on. And God again refused to give me over to despair. He deepened His imprint on my heart and He held on tightly when I was letting go. So…what does my relationship with God look like now? Well there has been growth of course. Five years ago, I lost everything. In past times, I would have seen this as a perfect example of Gods abandonment of me, that view would have made prayer repulsive to me. Whenever hard times hit me in the past, I avoided God. It drove me from Him instead of toward Him. In my soul, I was convinced that either He was causing this or He didn't care about it at all because if he did, He would have involved Himself by now. So I would avoid prayer and only seek Him when things were going well.

These last five years have been devastating financially. Yet, for the first time in my life, I actually seek God more than I ever have before. I awaken in the night, troubled and worried and I find myself seeking His presence and finding calm. He loves me! And I understand it now.

This present darkness will never consume us; His love will never reach an end. His grace has no limit and no boundary and there is nothing I can do to change that. My daddy is passionately in love with me and my circumstance has nothing to do with His love, nor is it an indicator of it or a measure for it. In his presence, I find safety from the storm raging outside and from the howling voice of the memories of failure and disappointment that will try to draw me back to doubt Him. His love has finally established itself as the bedrock of my soul and I will not be budged.

I have learned a very valuable lesson in these long, sometimes desperate years. That is that my walk with God is mine alone. I don't owe it to anyone to suffer, as they demand I suffer, or say what they want me to say, or shut off my tears and fake a smile because that is what they think Christianity demands. To do so is to be fraudulent and that helps no one. If anything has become true to me, it is that this age-old practice of faking it and hiding our pain in the name of proclaiming the Gospel is only serving to wound us deeper and isolate us more. So many men have reached out to me specifically because I have been honest about my hurts. My openness has made it safe for them to be open as well.

Jesus said He came not for the whole but for the sick. However, if no one wants to admit to being sick, how will you ever be healed? If you won't speak honestly about your pain, how will others ever find hope for *their* pain?

It's not the restoration that draws men to my story at first…it's the pain. It's the blood, sweat, and tears of hanging on by a thread, day after day after day with only enough faith to survive. There were times I used to wake up on my living room floor at 2 A.M. with my fingertips bleeding because I had cried myself to sleep in hurt and anger and was in such pain that I was pulling the carpet fibers until they cut my fingers. If I skip over that part of the story and only tell of joy and happiness I not only fail to bring hope, but I extinguish any hope they might already have.

There is an overwhelming sense of hopelessness in the early days and years after a divorce. To ignore it or make light of it is to invalidate the undeniable pain of the human heart. Jesus came to this world specifically to feel those hurts…not to avoid them. I learned the lesson of being honest. I refuse to alter my testimony to fit the caprices of a church or a man. I have a story to tell but if it isn't my story, it is no story. This is who I am. This is what my life was like as I walked through this dark valley and to leave out the most painful parts is to do great injustice to someone trying to decide if it is safe for him to open up. By revealing my doubts, fears, hurts, and pains and by being honest about how I doubted God and how angry I was with Him, I knock down the walls that keep others from being as honest. The truth is that Jesus never healed anyone who didn't admit they were in need of healing. Our churches today have forced us to whitewash our pain and filter our hurt so that we seem barely bruised when we are, in fact, deeply broken. I will never permit that in my life, or my ministry, again.

Gradually, over time. I learned that His love is bottomless and His application of it is relentless, and I am the richer for it. Perhaps most telling is how easily in prayer, the word "Father' can escape my lips. God is my father, and I get it now. He is no longer the distant, cold, mean spirited, rage filled father I was raised with. Nor is he the invisible, uncaring, rejecting, disconnected father I tried so hard to discover. He is all I ever dreamed of and longed for in my lifetime. He takes the model of my love for my daughter, wraps it in His perfection, multiplies it times infinity, and applies it in liberal doses to my soul. And each morning I awaken to find a fresh application of His love waiting for me, alongside those new mercies he speaks of. My daughter summed it up so perfectly at age four… *"My daddy always tells me He love me."* If you listen closely…even in your darkest hour and your deepest pain… your Daddy is always telling you He loves you too.

This chapter is entitled "Field of Dreams." Of course, this is a reference to the classic baseball movie of the 80's starring Kevin Costner and the great James Earl Jones. The premise of the story, for that one of you who has never seen it, is that Kevin Costner's character, Ray Kinsella, is a corn farmer in Iowa. One day he hears a voice saying, *"If you build it, he will come."* Over the course of the next few days, he comes to understand that "it" is a baseball field and "he" is Shoeless Joe Jackson, the great baseball player from the 1918 Chicago White Sox. Shoeless Joe had been banished from baseball for alleged gambling. He was also Ray Kinsella's fathers' favorite player and the focal point of the final argument Ray had with his father before he left home. We find out in the movie that Ray and his father had been at odds and were not speaking when he finally left for college. Sadly, before they could reconcile, Ray's father dies and Ray never got the chance to make things right.

So Ray plows under a good portion of his corn crop and constructs a small baseball field, complete with lights and some small bleachers, and then he waits. For months, nothing happens and his reputation as a lunatic is beginning to take shape in the town. Just when he is ready to give up and plant corn again on the site of the ball field, Shoeless Joe shows up. He comes strolling out of the corn, dressed in his White Sox uniform, almost as baffled by the events as Ray himself. The movie progresses to tell a wonderful tale about others who need the ball field to heal various wounds in their lives. A writer who became cynical toward his favorite sport when his beloved Brooklyn Dodgers moved to Los Angeles and they tore down Ebbet's Field. A young man who played one half inning in the big leagues before being sent back to the minors, and who could not bear the thought of another season wandering the countryside in a beat-up bus, waiting for the call up. He quit baseball and became a beloved family doctor in a small Minnesota town...but deep inside he longed for one chance to face a big league pitcher. He loved his life as it was...but he always wondered "what if." He too found his opportunity to redeem something missing from his life when he stepped foot on the ball field of Ray Kinsella.

The movie rolls along and it seems like everyone finds the one thing they were searching for in their life is somehow fulfilled in that little baseball field cut into a corn crop...everyone except Ray Kinsella. He comes to understand that it wasn't for Shoeless Joe that he built the field. It wasn't just for Terrance Mann, (James Earl Jones' character) the writer from the 60's who gave up baseball in bitterness because of the loss of his childhood team. And it wasn't for Dr. Archibald, "Moonlight" Graham, played magnificently by Burt Lancaster, who had spent his life wondering if he could have hit major league pitching but who comforted himself in the love of a small town for their local doctor.

The final scene is one that I cannot watch, to this day some 20 years after the film was released, without tearing up. The ghost players have finished their games for the day and they are packing up their gear. By this point, the roster has grown to about 40 of the greatest players in baseball history who have long ago passed away but have returned to this magical field. Ray begins to question aloud why he bothered with this project. There is still some great-unanswered question burning within him and he can't even figure out what it is, much less find the answer. Shoeless Joe turns to him in that moment and says *"if you build it...he will come"* and as he says this he nods toward an unnamed catcher at home plate, removing his protective equipment and packing up. In that, instant Ray has his epiphany, he stares at the man in silence for a moment...Ray's wife Annie joins him at his side and she asks, *"What is it Ray?"* Finally able to speak he says, *"Oh my God...it's my father."* He recognizes the man behind home plate as his father...a much younger version than Ray ever knew. His dad had at one time been a minor league catcher in the Yankees organization. His father walks up to him and the viewer is not sure if he knows he is looking at his son. But Ray knows, and he is stunned. The turmoil inside him is palpable. Does he reveal his identity? What does he say? The elder Kinsella thanks him for providing this beautiful field where these guys can come to play once more. He is introduced to Ray's wife and young daughter, and in that moment Ray almost introduces the man as little Karen's grandfather but something makes him hold back. Maybe it is all too good to be true or maybe his own pain from never having had the chance to say goodbye have overwhelmed him. For whatever reason, Ray can't quite speak the words "Father" or "Dad." The elder Kinsella remarks how beautiful this place is and asks if it might be heaven. "No" responds Ray "it's Iowa." Ray then asks haltingly, *"Is there a heaven?"* and his father replies, *"Yes...it's the place where dreams come true"* Ray then responds *"Then I guess this is heaven."* The elder turns to walk toward the cornfield, the portal through which these ghosts pass to and from this ballpark. Suddenly Ray asks him, voice trembling… *"Hey…dad…you wanna have a catch?"* The elder turns around and with great relief on his face, he says, *"yes…I'd like that."*

In that moment, you knew he was aware all along whom Ray was and he was awaiting Ray's response to his presence. The final scene is a zoom to pan of Ray Kinsella throwing a baseball with his dad, whatever harsh words had passed between them now long forgotten, only a father and a son enjoying each others presence. My own life was like this final scene. I was hurting, bruised, battered, and cynical. Like Terrance Mann, I had lost hope and the belief in the things I loved, and the things that brought me joy. Situations arose, people had let me down, and I closed up shop and became cold and isolated instead of writing it off to the human condition and finding myself a new team to cheer.

Like Moonlight Graham, I was longing for a return to my childhood dreams and the vision I had believed in for my life. Having lost everything to a divorce, I was always wondering what might have happened if I had stayed married, if Holly had more patience with our situation and we had lasted through our difficult start. I seemed content on the outside but inside, in my quiet moments I wondered how life might have been if I had done things a little differently.

I was like Ray Kinsella; my relationship with my father had been damaged because of stupid lies and deceptions I had believed in and now, years later, my own fatherhood was teaching me the truth about my heavenly Father. However, by this time, so much had happened and so much time had passed that I wasn't sure how to approach Him now that I had the chance. He responded in the same unassuming non-intrusive way the elder Kinsella did in the movie. Like Ray, having a catch with his dad, so much of my time now is spent just sitting quietly sensing His presence around me and feeling His love in my heart. It is wonderful and I cannot even grasp how I survived those dark years without this mercy and grace. There is no secret to it. I didn't commit a certain number of verses to memory or say a certain prayer. I certainly read a few books on the topic, Brennan Manning's work being top on my list, but that wasn't what finally cracked the block of ice that encased me. It was simply the passing of time and God moving and countering my moves, like a chess game, toward the final place where He would hold me in checkmate.

I couldn't run, I couldn't hide, I was finally in a place where He could rain His love on me until it broke through, and I grasped it. When you are finally there, there isn't anything for you to do, except throw your hands up and surrender to Him. Give Him time and opportunity and He will pursue you until you fall and then He will pounce on you and smother you with His love. Your father loves you and all He needs to prove it is a chance. If you build it…He will come.

Chapter 14

Behold all Things Become New

This is the part I've waited for...

...Writing all that has proceeded has been cathartic for me, and deeply moving. Let me say here and now that looking back in this manner has shown me how gracious and loving, God has been. There were so many nights when I thought I would have been better off dead rather than hurting the way I was. But God is faithful. He has broad shoulders. For all the wrath and bile I spit at Him during this ordeal, He never responded with anything but love, kindness, healing, and mercy. He was my balm in Gilead and he healed my wounds.

Wounds are strange things. First, they hurt, then they annoy, and then we actually wear them like badges of honor. I have a knot on my lip where I was hit in the mouth with a puck in a men's hockey league back home about 20 years ago. When it happened, it hurt like mad. Then it was annoying because it was a big knot for a long time and it curled my lip downward into a snarl. Now it's barely perceptible and so it makes for great "war stories." I have other scars too. I have a nasty one on my left thumb where I wasn't careful enough on a job site and laid it on a table saw. It's every bit as nasty as it sounds. I had 13 stitches in one inch on my thumb. I have had three surgeries on my right shoulder and while the scars are very big, and the surgeries hurt like crazy, I rather dig it when someone asks me about them.

We men are weird that way. However, I am finding that emotional wounds are different. Soul wounds don't show themselves outwardly, unless you know what you are looking for. And our society has this very unsettling, "deal with it already and move on!" attitude about it. I think that is why the Bible says, "Man looks on the outward appearance but God looks on the heart." I know that was a reference to people who put on airs and pretense, but I think too, it tells us that God sees what men cannot, or will not. I believe we all have access to the eyes of the Spirit if we ask for it. We could all see our damaged hurting friends if we chose to. However, that sort of wound is hard to look at, because we know how to heal physical hurts, but we don't know what to do for a wounded soul. And sadly, for whatever reason, we forget that The Great Physician isn't just a healer of the flesh, but of the Spirit and the soul even more so.

I was recently watching a special on returning vets from the Iraq war and the amazing advances made in prosthetic limbs. Now, right here and now, let me say I am not implying whatsoever that a highly developed prosthetic can take the place of ones own body, but they have come a long, long way. We see men and women running marathons with one or both legs having been replaced with prosthetics. Medicine is doing more each day and making greater strides in this field. However, there is no prosthetic for the heart. There is no synthetic replacement for the soul. They have no artificial dreams they can implant when the ones you've had for as long as you can remember are shattered. Hearts break and souls are crushed, dreams die, and there isn't a man alive who can alter that fact. Nor is there a man or woman alive who can repair or replace them. That is the realm of the One who made them in the first place. And this is His chapter.

It began one night in a church service. I was so broken and so hurting and so lost in my sorrow. As the worship music played, I was talking to God in my heart. *"What is wrong with me Lord?" I asked silently. "Why can't I let all this go and be healed?" "Why can't I praise you anymore, why can't I worship you like I once did?"* I got no immediate reply. Nothing but dark silence. The preacher opened the altar for prayer and I stood still, not wanting to move. Another verse was sung and another and finally I walked out of my aisle and knelt at the altar. I don't even remember what the worship singers were singing. In my heart, God was showing me a vision. I could feel Jesus walking by me, just ahead of where I was kneeling. I could not see Him, but I sensed Him and I had a vision in my heart of His robes, just out of the reach of my extended fingers.

Suddenly I was praying the words to "Pass me not oh Gentle Savior." I could visualize His robes touching me lightly, like the woman with the issue of blood, and I was straining to reach the hem of his garment. The words to a song my friend had written were ringing in my heart... "But let your hem brush my head and I will be free..." I asked God, "Lord what is wrong with me? And suddenly He answered, *"Son you have a broken heart."* I said *"No duh*

Lord" or something to that effect. *"I've had a broken heart for years now…how can we heal it?"* Then He said something to me that tore me asunder…" *No Son…you have a broken heart…it doesn't work anymore. It is broken"* *"You don't feel, you don't weep, you don't laugh, and you have no joy at all.* " *Your heart…your very inner man is broken and it doesn't function anymore"* At that very instant as God was whispering those very words into my heart; I felt an arm on each shoulder. Two men from the church were kneeling, one on either side. The one man spoke; *"James we need to pray for Craig, he has a broken heart"* then they prayed for me prayed for me and every word poured over me like medicine. The man who prayed knew nothing of what I was going through and yet his prayer was so specific and so precise that it was obviously from God. Then the other man prayed for me for areas we had talked about and for areas, I had never revealed to him in our chats. God showed up that night and started repairing my heart.

I am in tears as I write this even now, eight years later. I wept at the altar and told those men what had just happened. This was the beginning. God started a work that day that took Him another 6 years to complete. And in reality, He is still doing the work. What God began that night was the literal re-creation of my heart and soul. You see they can't put a different one in you. Man can't replicate that part of you. They can give you a prosthetic leg so you can walk again and a prosthetic arm so you can function again, but when your heart is shattered, and your soul is in pieces, only one physician can replace that. The

One who made it in the first place. The wonderful thing is that He doesn't use a synthetic creation that is a decent replacement but far from perfect. He re -creates what He intended for you to have all along. He did it for me that night. It has taken more time, many more tears but the work had started, and it gave me a glimmer of hope that one day, I would feel and love, and laugh, and praise and worship again.

Six years later, all that has been done in me. There are men reading this that are no doubt in tears right now, because I just described you. It has been years since you felt, since you laughed, since you smiled or had a light heart. This terrible battle has stripped you of all emotion and you are mechanical now, unfeeling, and cold. Maybe you throw yourself into your job to avoid anyone seeing this side of you. Maybe you isolate yourself from others as often as possible because you don't want to be seen as the guy with no smile and no sense of humor. Maybe you are like me. I was the consummate class clown in high school. If it would bring a laugh, I would do it. By the time, I was 40 I was the least funny guy in the room. My broken, unfeeling heart would not permit it. So I avoided any situation that reminded me of who I used to be.

Maybe there is even a guy out there right now who, like me, slips out to the bathroom during praise and worship at your church, rather than sticking out like a sore thumb because your sorrow so consumes you. To you I say there is hope. The bad news isn't really bad news.

Your heart is broken. I know Who can fix it. Listen to me broken man…Your Daddy loves you. He sees the dense fog of pain and hurt you are in. He knows you can't feel anything anymore. He longs to bring the color back to your canvas and the warm breeze of summer to your winter-chapped face.

Perhaps you are like me, without an earthly dad who could put his arm around you and reassure you that it will be okay. Let me tell you, you have a Heavenly Father who loves you. He is the Giver of Life. Not just once, at the Cross-, but daily. You can live again. You will feel again. It starts with you…all you need to do is open your heart to Him. Pour it out to your Father God. Don't hold back. He knows anyway. He heard every hurtful word you shouted at Him in your most painful moments, and He never once judged you for them. He wept with you when you wept, and He kept weeping when you could no longer weep. He loves you and wants you to come home to Him. Crawl into His arms and let him kiss your face and love on you. Let His love start a fire burning in your broken soul again. Regardless of what you might think or feel, you have not gone too far for His love, grace, and restoration to reach you. He has counted every tear and He holds them dear to His heart. His word says He "heals the brokenhearted and binds up their wounds." He binds up their wounds. He opens the old bandages that we try to put on ourselves, He looks straight on at the wounds we carry, he pours in His love and healing, then he wraps them up in clean bandages, and makes us better than we were before. He "restores my soul." How many times have you read that verse from Psalm 23? It is time to *believe* it. He restores my soul!" When my soul was laid waste, empty, and broken, He restored it. He made it like new.

I've had people come to me in church and ask me what has happened. I don't say that to boast, I say that because only a few years ago I was so angry and so hurting and so broken inside that I would literally leave the sanctuary during Praise and worship. Men, He can and He will do the same for you. Bring Him your broken heart. Lay the pieces at his feet. Open your soul, weep, cry out, reach out, or lay in silence. *But come to Him.* He has the healing for what only He can heal. He understands the hurt you feel. He longs to take your pain and your hurt and replace it with something so beautiful that words can barely describe. There is hope. Hope for your life and quite possibly hope for your marriage if it is not too late.

Most men reading this will have already progressed to the point that it would take God and Him alone to save their marriage. But think about that statement for a moment. It would take God to save it…well why let it go that far? Go to God first. Why do we always wait until it is beyond what we can fix? Why don't we go to Him first? In my case, it was because I was too ashamed of what had already happened in my marriage to think that God would bother getting involved, and because I knew it would require me to take responsibility for my failures and shortcomings and leave Holly's up to God. It takes a double portion of His grace to swallow your pride so completely that you choose to stop defending yourself when your wife is telling you all that is wrong with you, (assuming it's true and not abusive) and simultaneously choose not to continue the battle by listing all her shortcomings.

Proverbs says, "A soft answer turns away wrath" but it very hard to answer softly when your pride wants to scream, and fight back. It is difficult to "do kindness to your enemy and so heap coals of fire on her head" when your human nature wants to go straight to "an eye for an eye." What I know now, too late for my marriage, is that had I drawn closer to Jesus, become more and more like Him, and asked Him for the wisdom to know how to answer my wife when she was trying to wound me, we might have survived our hard times. Had I depended on Him to fix what was broken and not tried to do it all myself in a vain attempt to save my pride and prove my manhood, I wouldn't even be writing this right now. I know this for sure.

Now I'm not promising anyone who reads this that it's some sort of panacea for whatever ails your home life, but I do know that God desperately wants to heal your marriage and make your family something that reflects His glory and blessing. It starts with you, man. One thing I see much of when I talk to men going through separation or divorce is the desire to fix it all at once. We find ourselves in a terrible mess and our wife has left or is threatening to leave. And we want to do what men always do…fix years of damage in ten minutes. We tell our wives, (and ourselves) that if we can just knock it out of the park on this next try, everyone will be happy and they will forget the big disappointment our last three strikeouts caused. The truth is, we strain harder and harder with each strike out until are so tense from trying and failing that we couldn't even bunt anymore…much less launch a home run. The "fans" begin to expect our mighty three swings and no contact before we even get up to bat. And after we fail predictably, we sulk back to the dugout and make excuses about a blown call, and begin the cycle of telling ourselves, and our family, how we will hit one next time, and everything will be okay. But next time doesn't come, or by the time it does, we are so far behind in the score that it doesn't matter. Instead of a highlight from a victory, it is a footnote in another loss.

We have to get out of the thinking that tells us we have to instantly fix everything we did wrong for the last (fill in the blank) years and this is difficult. It requires us to be honest with ourselves and with our spouse. We can no longer hurriedly tell her how we will be all right as soon as we get up to bat again. She has seen your swing. You don't even have warning track power anymore. Try for a single and see what happens. Maybe at first nothing. But string together a few singles and a run crosses the plate, and maybe along with it your wife perks up and takes notice. Add to the score a few times and before you know it, there is excitement on the bench and peace in the clubhouse.

Men…Peter was a failure the first few times he tried serving Jesus. But God specializes in using and blessing failures. Remember, as the great Zig Ziglar always said; "Failure is an event…not a person." Moses blew it in the desert in a moment of anger. Elijah got depressed. David committed adultery and then murder to cover it up…and he was "the apple of God's eye." Why do you think you have to do it better than they did? Pick yourself up, dust yourself off, set a couple of realistic goals, and swing away. Get that first single and build on it. As Paul said, "forget those things which are behind" If forgiveness is in order, ask for it. You will not fix your marriage in one fell swoop. And you cannot get your wife to move at your pace. You are dealing with two distinct wills in a divorce. Reconciliation is only possible when both wills desire it. The more you try to force change, the deeper you will sink in the quicksand. It may be humbling, it may be difficult, you may have to tear everything down and rebuild from the very foundation, but trust me when I tell you…that is better than having nothing left at all to build on. It is humbling, it is hard, it goes against everything society tells us about quick fixes…but it is God's way and it works. I learned, much too late, that all I can do is take care of *my* stuff. God had to take care of Holly's. I could not force her to be something she did not desire to be, no matter how I tried.

You can only take responsibility for your part of the problems. Then leave it to God.

Chapter 15

"God, are You Sure

You're in Control?"

I am old enough to remember Vietnam...

and especially the years after. One of the common complaints from both the sideline observer and the soldiers who fought was that nobody listened to the guy in the jungle. We have heard it a thousand times... "If they would have fought that war the right way we could have been done in six weeks." I don't know if that's really the case, but I understand the notion. What it implies is that the people who run wars, and most importantly, the people who have the ability to influence the outcome of a war, are distant and unaffected. Some General in Washington isn't watching his friends die in battle and so he makes decisions based on numbers and political objectives.

That's how it appears at least. About a million times during my divorce and in the years afterwards, I shouted a form of the same question at God. I peppered it with salty language and screamed it until my voice broke and my throat hurt. I was angry and wounded and I felt like God had abandoned me to my pain, sorrow, fear, and loneliness. When I screamed, "Where ARE You?" I was afraid He had abandoned me. When I yelled, "Why don't You get in the middle of this and fix it? Why don't you just bring her back?" I was really afraid He was rejecting me and that the entire divorce and subsequent pain was all His doing and all because of some cosmic decision He had made. This was my lot in life and He was behind it all...otherwise He would have waved His hand, used His infinite power, and changed everything in a blink. When I shouted, "Why have you done this to me?" I was afraid He had allowed the entire series of events in response to some bad thing I had done, or some area of my life I had failed.

I reasoned in my heart that God must not love me because He said He is a better father than I ever could be, and I surely would not let my little girl feel this kind of pain. I heaped a thousand false accusations upon His shoulders and He never once rejected me because of it. When I was screaming "God where are You" I wasn't waiting long enough to hear the answer. His being in my problem meant, to my mind, Him doing what I wanted when I wanted it. Unless He was acting as I declared He should, and healing my marriage and restoring my family, than I had decided He wasn't there. It wasn't fair to God and it wasn't the truth. The truth is that Jesus said "Lo I am with you always" He was with Peter both on top of the mountain when the He was speaking with Moses and Elijah and when He was raising Lazarus, and just as much when He was being dragged from the garden by a posse and beaten by guards. He was in all of those situations and He was the same powerful Lord and Savior. It's just that both victory and defeat were part of God's plan and Jesus knew that. I had to learn it and because I really didn't want to, it took a long time. I can tell you this, men; God is in the middle of your hurt. He does understand. Jeremiah 29:11 is *never* a lie. He *always* knows the plans He has for you and they are always plans for good and for blessing. It may be a thorny path to get there and you may lose sight of Him. That period of feeling abandoned might even go on for a long while, what St. John of the Cross called "The Long Dark Night of the Soul." Make no mistake…God is in your circumstance. The second He abandons you to your situation is the second He becomes a liar, and we know that can't happen.

Sometimes, that knowledge will be all you can cling to, but cling anyway. God is near. When I was screaming, "Why don't you get in the middle of this and fix it" what I really was saying was "I am afraid You are going to permit this and I want you to fix it my way." For so long I was so mad at God for not fixing my marriage. I could have thrown a hundred verses at you about how God could change this person's heart and that person's heart. He hardened Pharaoh and then he softened Pharaoh. He "turns the kings' heart like the course of a river" Proverbs tells us. Yet He could not, or more directly, He *would not*, magically change my wife's heart and make her stop this whole painful disaster. Why? That was the question I had for Him and I didn't much like His answers. What was so funny was I knew the truth…I even explained it to my daughter.

She was about four when she asked me for the first time, "Why God didn't make Mommy stop the divorce?" I told her, very carefully, about free will, and How God doesn't just go around making people do what is right.

She grasped it, but I refused. I wrestled with Him over that one for years. Maybe I thought I could change His mind about it. Then I finally got to a place where I could admit that I was quite mistreated by her and while God never ordains divorce, He certainly ordains two married people treating each other with decency and respect. That was hard for me to admit. I wanted to, and did for a long time; take 100% of the blame. I dragged that burden around with me like a ball and chain. When I finally could admit to myself that she had sinned against me as well, and it was 50% her fault, I felt guilty.

Men need to realize a few important facts. In almost no circumstance is it all your fault. I say almost, because I am sure there are those infrequent examples of the longsuffering wife who finally ceases to cope with a monster of a husband and decides to divorce. (I know of one such situation personally, so it does happen) For the most part, it's about 50/50. In fact, I have observed that most marriages don't end because of the problems; they end because one person chooses an entirely different way of dealing with the problems than the other. Men...we have already established the necessity of admitting you were wrong...now lets establish the fact that you need to admit you were wronged.

Unless you are one of the exceptions, and your wife should have left you, then you are going to have to lift your own foot off your neck and let yourself up off the mat. Let me share something very profound God showed me on one very contemplative Maundy Thursday. Remember when Jesus told Peter he would deny Him three times before the rooster crowed the next morning? Peter went out and did exactly that, with gusto. Cursing, swearing, and reviling God, he swore on oath that he didn't know Jesus. It was tragic and crushing and it tears out my heart because I have done no less than Peter on far too many occasions.

But the morning of Maundy Thursday, God showed me the same story in a new light. I can't say it was a vision, but while in prayer that day, Jesus spoke to me and showed me the same scene…only I was Peter. He said to me; "when you deny my love for you, when you refuse to accept me for what I am, and refuse to let Me love you as I desire, then you deny me as Peter did." He continued, "When you will not see yourself as I see you, and when you shrink from me in shame instead of rushing to my side and letting me fellowship with you, then you deny me as well. If you can't accept me as I say I am, then you deny me. I cannot be anything less or other than I have said I am"

For years, I ran from His love for me. I punished myself for failing in my marriage and I let my ex wife beat up on me even after the divorce as some way to "pay for my sins." Men, when you do that, you sin against your Savior! He paid such a terrible price to secure your salvation and when you let people treat you as anything less than one of His, you offend His love for you, and you cheapen the price He paid. My favorite author is Brennan Manning. Brennan likes to say it like this; "The greatest act of love I can offer Jesus is to let Him love me" Christ's commandment to forgive others starts with the presupposition that you have forgiven yourself and accepted Christ's forgiveness. Start now, walking as a cherished, loved, restored, accepted son who has failed no more or no less than any other son has. The Bible reminds us…it's Christ in you, the hope of glory.

Finally, here is the painful point. I would often fall on my knees and bellow; "God why have you done this to me?" I could not bring myself to accept the fact that I had been sinned against just as much as I sinned against Holly. I could not let myself believe that Jesus was actually allowing this to happen. So in my pain and anguish I arrived at a monstrous conclusion…He was actually doing this to me. This could not be an act of the will alone. Something this painful had to be on purpose. It's insane now, but at the point of my deepest hurt, it seemed plausible. I could come up with no other reason for the events that ruined my life. God didn't allow it because after all, he hates divorce and there were all those verses decrying divorce. He didn't leave it to chance because that would have rendered Him powerless and I needed Him to be powerful. My argument about free will was falling on my own deaf ears. No, the only thing I could think of was He hated me and He was doing this to me. Maybe to even some cosmic score or to punish me for not being a perfect husband or maybe it was a generational curse. Whatever reason He refused to act like God, (as I determined He should) and he did this to me.

For a while, I believed this and it turned me into "Lieutenant Dan" from Forrest Gump. I was climbing the mast and shaking my fist at him. Sitting there on the blown off stump of a heart I had inside me railing at Him for all I was worth. The story has already been related earlier about how he healed my truly broken heart. It took a while. Here is what I learned. Men…He doesn't hate you. He can't. He also doesn't do anything evil to His children. The Bible teaches the exact opposite. But, in His infinite wisdom, He long ago chose to allow free will on earth. The fact is that free will often results in pain to those who find themselves caught in its wake.

My wife was not happy…she made some choices long before she chose to divorce me. She chose not to forgive my shortcomings. She chose to be hateful and harmful instead of gracious. She chose to remind me of all I was not and helped me feel even worse about it. Then she chose to divorce me instead of trying to make it work. I chose to react badly and sinfully, I chose to try to fix it with my own power and limited wisdom, and I chose to make bad decision after bad decision in some dead-end effort to fix everything at once. Both of us chose poorly but she ultimately chose to end it. Nothing I could have done would have stopped it by then.

My attorney gently reminded me of this when he told

me to stop contesting it. "Craig" he said, "I can keep taking your money as long as you want me to, but ultimately she will get this divorce because this is a no-fault state." He explained further, "The only reason she needs to get a divorce, is that she wants the divorce" I was contesting it because I felt to do otherwise would make me guilty of violating every commandment against divorce. I was wrong. Jesus said, "Listen… I am with you all the time." He is residing within you, so why would He harm you? If Christ in you is the hope of glory, than for Christ to harm you or intend evil for you would be intending evil for Himself. Accept His love for you and realize you are wounded too. He cares, He knows, He wants to heal your broken heart and bind up your wounds. It is okay to admit that it hurt you and that it wasn't all your fault.

Chapter 16

The Victorious Limp...

Finding something good in it all

For a very long time…

…it was hard for me to point to anything that came about as a result of my divorce and call it good. How can pain be thought of as a positive? Especially the kind of crushing pain that divorce brings. As years have gone by, and as I have surrendered, as best I could, the situation to God, He has caused some good fruit to come from the broken ground of my soul. Many things come to mind. I think for me, the most prominent fruit that has been borne in my heart has come because of the time I spend missing my daughter. I see her on Tuesdays for 5 hours and every other weekend. Then in the summer, she lives with me full time and goes to her mom's on that schedule. I try to find time each week to go to her school and have lunch with her at least once. I have done this since Pre School and it makes her feel very special, that her dad comes to see her. Usually I will bring some little magic trick to impress her friends. They all think I am the coolest dad and it gives her a little boost of pride. To me, (as my hero Brian Piccolo once said) "There is nothing more fun than a little kid," so I enjoy it too.

God used my intense love for Morgan to show me…slowly I must admit…how much He loves me and desires to be with me. He has shown me how broken His heart is when I don't take the time to be in His Presence. I am not talking about structured prayer or Bible study either. I am talking about spending time with my Father, hanging out…doing what fathers and sons do. I spend time with Him in my woodshop building furniture. I spend time with Him sitting in my study playing guitar and writing songs. I spend time with Him when I am posting on my blog, or even during the time I have been writing this book. I especially feel His presence when I am playing hockey. If it brings me joy, He wants to do it with me. Aren't we all like that with our kids?

My daughter loves to ride her bike. She loves to ride with me. Now I must admit that I would prefer to ride about 50 miles at a time, in silence, with little or no stopping. My daughter, however, wants to ride to the playground and stop for a swing or two. She stops frequently and a bike ride to her is a slow tour of the neighborhood. But to me, this time is priceless. I ride with her whenever she asks, if possible. Because the real point is being with her. Not every bike ride has to be an object lesson or a teaching tool. I don't have to apply some mystical spiritual truth to each time we pedal down the block. All either of us wants is to be with the other, that is all God really wants.

Life will demand plenty of active, anguished prayers and supplication. There will be nights when you will cry out until dawn because of some pain you are in, some need you, or someone else might have. He is certainly there for that. But what He desires from us mostly is to come into His presence and just sit there. Let Him be loving toward us. Most of the time this is done in silence. I have discovered His presence in the most unlikely places. Hiking through the woods. Sitting on Bethany Beach at sunrise. Walking with my daughter on that same beach under a full moon on summer vacation. And especially when I am on the ice. It may surprise you to know that I feel God's loving presence very specifically when I am playing hockey with my friends here in Nashville. Why? Because my father loves me! And it makes Him very happy to see me happy. I have friends who find their greatest times of communion with God when they are in the field hunting. The point is my separation from Morgan taught me how painful that same separation is to God when it happens between Him and me. There have been moments when that pain has been so strong and cut so deep that I thought I would die. I have cried myself to sleep more than once missing my little princess. God loves me no less…and misses me far more. Take your pain and loneliness, and the anguish you feel and picture God feeling that way when you don't spend time with Him. You have a choice…your time with God is not dictated by a court or a divorce decree. It's up to you and me. We can choose to set aside moments each day to give Him, and in those moments allow Him the relationship He desires with us…and in those same moments we redeem the sadness we feel when we long for our children.

Every struggle and every sorrow is a potential lesson learned. In the years after my divorce, I struggled terribly with shame. I was ashamed to have failed in marriage, regardless of who did what to whom. When I would go to church, I felt like a thousand eyes were on me, noticing my "alone-ness." I felt as if everyone could see straight into my sorrow and my shame. I felt *different.* I wasn't married anymore. Of course, the enemy of our souls had a field day with this. He would whisper in my ear all the things I was afraid of. *"They must think I'm some sort of wife-beater, or they must think I cheated on her, or they must think I was a monster / couldn't hold a job / was a lousy dad…* "You name it, I thought it. It was isolating and painful. It is amazing how often I have relayed that story and had a look of relief come across the faces of men who I am talking to. They have all felt the same things. The first time a man walks into his home church after he gets divorced is very hard. If you let God use this, He will open doors of opportunity for you.

These days I notice others who have the same lost, pained look on their faces. I pray for them of course, but I might find myself going to them and putting an arm around them and just letting them know I understand. Remember this to…your friends are very bewildered right now. Most of my friends didn't know what to say to me after my divorce. They didn't know how much pain I was in…was I happy it was over with, was I angry? Would asking me about it unleash a torrent of sorrow they could not be comfortable with? Here is a sad truth I learned through all of it…and I will catch flak for saying this but it is true. Everyone will tell you they care and they are "here for you"…but few people really mean that. At least not in the way you need them to. You will find that God will reveal one or two people who really get it, and will listen repeatedly and immerse themselves in your situation and see you through. Most other folks are so uncomfortable with it, and quite honestly…so busy with their own lives, that they will tell you they are praying for you as they brush past you on their way out the door.

That's life…get used to it. I was blessed with about 4 men who were willing to bear with hearing the same stories over and over, willing to call me up and ask me to dinner, or a ball game or a movie, knowing full well it was going to entail dealing with my sorrow on some level. I had many who meant well but did little.

I am indicting no one with these statements. Not everyone has a gift for empathy. A scant few had the ability to imagine themselves in my shoes and gave me the kind of loving friendship they would appreciate if they were ever in my position. So the challenge is twofold…

Number One: remember that God is where you really need to go with your grief. He is limitless in His patience and understanding. He will never grow tired of your entreaties for mercy in this time of grieving.

He knows you better than your closest friend does and He will never leave you nor forsake you, as He promised. Jesus said, "Yes I am with you forever!" That includes times of sorrow and loneliness when you feel abandoned.

Number Two: Search out opportunities to be the kind of friend to some other divorced man that you needed at your darkest hour. If you are a journal keeper, make sure you write down even your most painful emotions; share them with the next guy who walks this path. Let him know he isn't alone in his suffering and he isn't feeling something foreign to another Christian man. Let him know its okay to admit the pain he is in. You might want to approach your pastor about being available to assist him in counseling men in your church who face divorce. You will be amazed how much healing comes when you tell your story honestly, and God uses your honesty to minister to another man. If you've found a book that has helped you, or heard a sermon, or been to a conference or rented a movie, or heard a song…no matter how seemingly trivial, if something was used by God to touch you, make a note of it and share it.

When I was a little boy, my grandmother used to listen to southern gospel music. Now I will be the first to admit I would rather have bamboo shoots pushed under my fingernails than listen to that genre. But while I was writing this book, one song she used to really like, played over in my mind. It was called "Leave a Well in the Valley." The chorus goes like this; "Leave a well in the valley, the dark and lonesome valley; others have to walk that valley too. What a blessing when they find the well of joy you've left behind; leave a well in the valley you go through." Learn to dig wells in the moments of your deepest suffering, as you walk your darkest valley. Pray that if you must suffer, you suffer well. Make sure you learn every lesson… and feel every loss. Ask that not one opportunity for Christ's healing is missed in your pain. God will never let you suffer in vain, but He will bring about some good, if you surrender it to Him. Remember, everything He does in our lives is motivated by love.

I suppose the natural question that one would be inclined to ask right now is how can I be writing a book like this after seeing all the pain I was in? How could I even find the strength to find something positive enough in all of this to write about? What good came from this and how could God use this for His glory? Well those are fair questions, and especially since I realize that the majority of readers will be divorced men, I need to answer them thoroughly. We have a promise in scripture that tells us that whatever the enemy does to us with the intention of harming us, God will use for our blessing if we surrender it. The key is surrendering it and that is very difficult. We all tend to want to grasp our problems in a death grip and make them obey our will. Quite frequently, that forces God to the sidelines, waiting for us to hit bottom, give up, and loosen our grip. In that brokenness He steps in and takes over and makes it right, but getting there is a long road and not without pain. To be able to look back over the years and not just utter some platitudes about God using it for His glory but to actually mean it, is a miracle in itself. I didn't even like God for a good portion of the first eight years after my divorce years; much less believe He was at work in my behalf when I thought He was abandoning me. But He was. In reality He was working in His own behalf, because He knew, being wise and all that, that if He could get a hold of this mess and make something from it that brought Him glory and honor, then it would bring me my healing and blessing as a result.

How can God be glorified in my pain and sorrow? The simple answer is by my surrendering it to Him and Him empowering me not to act like a jerk. That is simple enough but it goes a whole lot deeper than that. God doesn't just throw a patch on us and give us the grace to "shut up and deal with it." That is not victory; that is survival. Homeless people who live under bridges have also learned to "shut up and deal with it." They deal with it by believing the lie completely until they not only accept the home under the bridge or in a box, but they embrace it. It becomes their last vestige of identity. Sometimes that need for identity keeps them from going to a shelter on the coldest night...because in the shelter they are reminded that they aren't special, they are, in fact, just another homeless guy. Another nothing in a sea of nothings. They are reminded of this every time they catch their own reflections in a storefront window. They have bought the lie and it now defines them. That is accepting your fate without a whimper and living in the mire with the pigs. That is not God using it for His glory, nor is it His will for you.

God grabs a hold of our situations and gathers up all the little pieces. Then He gives it thought and looks at what we have given Him to work with. He fixes this, reshapes that, corrects this flaw, seals this crack, recreates this base, heals this broken heart, binds up that wound...and suddenly something new and whole exists. Not a cracked work with a cheap repair, but a whole re-creation of our life. A new use and a new plan. He takes our mess and says, "You know…I can do something with this. I know exactly where I can use this once it's ready." That has brought immense healing for me. To see myself not as a washed up, failed, embarrassing divorcee with a broken heart and a permanent limp that only signifies a last-place finish. Instead, I see myself becoming a completed, renewed, re-created, beautiful work of God's hand. He has not relegated me to His scrap heap, suitable only for second-class kingdom work. He has ordained a work for my life that *required* this path I have walked. I would not be who I am now if not for this painful journey. No book, no ministry, no story of healing, no shining light guiding other men who are drifting in their own blackness, nothing. I would just be another divorcee who wept a few tears, found himself a new wife, started a new family, and repeated the same cycle. Maybe God would find another person to pick up this work and maybe not, but whomever I was supposed to meet and minister to might have slipped through the cracks.

God has used these things to make me stronger than I ever was. Where I labored in the belief that He was distant and rejecting, and thereby tried to live my faith on my own strength, I now have learned how to depend on Him and believe in His promises. My prayer life has changed drastically because of this. Groveling petitions that echo with self-loathing and shame and sound like a bad AM radio preacher, are now replaced with the voice of a confident son, asking His Father to simply make good on His promises. No begging, no pleading. Just a talk between a Father and His son. I trust Him to do as He said, and He enjoys hearing my voice.

In a more practical sense, I am no longer so needy of a relationship that I would accept anything, and would be devastated if a date didn't work out. I've been to the gates of hell, so to speak. There isn't much hurt I haven't felt, I can handle a date not going well and a girl not wanting to see me. It is liberating and it allows me a clear head to make decisions about who I will date. One day it might lead me to marriage again and if so, I will enter it whole and healthy because I will truly see it as complementing me and completing me... *not defining me.*

Of course, some areas still need further healing. As of the writing of this book, still no relationship exists between my father and me. This hurts and the more years go by the more I fear it may never happen. I worry that someday I will get the call that he is gone and I have run out of opportunities. But I have come to accept the fact that I cannot control that. Like my divorce, his is a decision that is made by him alone and then thrust upon me. I have no say in his reaction to me, like I had none in Holly's decision to leave. That was done to me and I could only react.

Regardless of my fathers' stance toward me I have two great men who love, me in Bob and I had Poppa John until he went home to Heaven two years ago, but his imprint on my soul remains. I have a daughter who adores me and I her. I have family who embraces me without condition. Most of all I have the love of my Heavenly Father, and His relentless, bottomless, matchless love is my source of strength and hope. So from all these occurrences and life lessons, what is next?

I have surrendered them to God, and he has, and is, making great things come from them. He has healed, restored, reinvigorated, and renewed, but what is next? Now that the dark curtain is lifting and I am getting back to the real me, is this real me anything like the old real me? How have I changed and how am I still the same and how am I getting back to the same? Well I have rediscovered my sense of humor. I may not be the class clown I once was in high school but I have been having fun lately. Yep...real genuine fun. One of my connections that maintained through the years was my youth pastor from my teen years, Dave Lewis. Dave and his wife pastor a church in southern Alabama now and we have always stayed in touch. He was the first person to read a draft of this book and has encouraged me immensely. He told me of three men in his church going through various stages of divorce and he is actually using what I wrote here to develop a plan to minister to them.

Dave and I have always, since I was a teenager in high school, had a great relationship. He was my youth pastor and my coach in high school, and he is my friend. He has always found my torqued sense of humor very entertaining. He gets me, and that has always been a link for us. I hadn't told many jokes in the years I struggled in darkness but lately we've reverted to our old routines from high school and it has been such fun. In some ways, I am back…and it feels great.

Developing this book has been a godsend. I had long forgotten how much I love to communicate, particularly by the written word. It has brought life back to my soul and the hours fly by when I am creating. I have returned to my great love recently as well…hockey. My friend Patrick asked me to help him coaching his son's roller hockey team and I am so glad we could work out the schedule. I have missed coaching and I feel so alive when I am out there with these young kids, teaching them the game I love so much, breaking down the nuances into lessons they can really grasp. I love the game and I love seeing them having such a good time as their skills and subsequently their confidence, improves. That is the essence of a good coach and I cherish the role.

I mentioned before that I graduated from Liberty University last May 2012. I am beginning seminary in March with the hopes of expanding my ministry. I host a radio talk show for divorced dads on Blogtalk radio, called "Sometimes Daddies Cry." I continue to write my divorced dad blog and have been a guest on Huffpost Live on various occasions to discuss the topic of divorced dads.

One last, very practical example of the "Victorious Limp" is from my own life. When I was knee deep in my pain and sorrow, my friend Michael Korieba was willing to walk with me through some of the deepest valleys. Michael had been through his own painful divorce, saw all the signs, and knew just where I was on my path. More than anyone else, Michael knew what to say and when to remain silent. He knew because he'd been there. He had his own limp and by reaching out to me…it became victorious. My desire is to pass that on through this work, and help others get to the point where they can finally see the victory in their own wounds as well. It's just another example of one wounded man finding healing and then passing that healing on to another. It works because that is God's way.

Chapter 17

Johnny Comes Marching Home

I am sitting in my kitchen on Friday, January 25, 2013...

...The thought just hit me that I am beginning the final chapter to this book. I started writing this almost 8 years ago, got serious about it in 2007, and now it is finally nearing completion. To be honest, I wondered if I had what it took to see this thing through. My to-do list is full of half-completed tasks. But God kept bringing me back to this project. I would write some, rest a while, and write some more. The first portion was easy because it was little more than me telling my story, but the last few chapters were written very slowly. Mostly because I had to wait on God to show me what He wanted to say. I hope I have been listening closely enough and I didn't miss His voice.

When I started on my road over 13 years ago, I didn't think I would survive it. The pain was enormous and seemed to have no bottom. I felt alone and afraid. I ran from God because I thought it was all His doing. What I learned was not that it was His doing, but that my wrong thinking of Him caused me to see it that way. If I have learned anything in these 13 long years, I have learned that my Father loves me. He loves me. He adores me. He wants only the best for me. He wants me to be happy, healthy, and blessed. I have felt His great heart breaking for me, and I can look back and see how often I pushed Him away...and how tenderly He approached my damaged soul again and again.

I weep now as I write this because I finally get it. He

never left my side and even though I vented all my anger, frustration, hurt pain and rage on Him. I couldn't chase Him away. His love is, as Brennan Manning says, relentless. He pursued me until I ran out of running room and He doggedly tracked me down until I gave up and let Him love me. While it was certainly within His power to free me from my sorrow and sadness with one wave of His hand, He chose a much more difficult path. Yet with it's sorrow, it is a path that leads to far greater blessing than I could ever fathom, and a far greater understanding of His love and grace and mercy than I had before all this took place. I can honestly say that had it not been for my divorce, more specifically had it not been for the way He used it once I surrendered it, I may not have ever grasped His mercy, and what it means when He says they are new every morning.

It has been for my good and not for my harm…even though Satan intended it that way. I have met my Father on this road…and He loves me. He never once left my side even when I told Him to, and He never once turned His back on me even though I turned mine on Him. He was exactly what, deep in my heart, I had hoped He would be. It took all this to find that out. If I have a final word to you men going through this it would be…Hope. Hope in Christ. Hope in a God who loves you, a God who feels your hurts and longs to heal you. He heals the brokenhearted and binds up their wounds. You need some hope right now. Believe me, I know.

And remember there are others watching. Your

friends, your church family, and especially your children. I am so glad that God walked me through this before my daughter was very old. She has seen her Daddy go from being sad and hurting all the time, to being happy and content in Christ. My greatest fear was turning into a bitter old man, and teaching her that when things happen that break your heart, God doesn't care and there is no hope. Instead she has seen God's love, shed abroad in our hearts. You are not alone, you are not forsaken, and you are not condemned. God loves you and He is seeking you right now, this instant. My prayer is you can drink deeply from this well I leave here with you. The war is over, weary soldier.

It's time to come home.

A Word After...

When I first submitted this manuscript to a literary agent friend, I thought it was finished then. I had poured my heart and soul into it and I didn't want to change anything at all. I had been quite convinced that this was Gods work and I was just the scribe. When he responded so positively to me I was a little shocked. He is, after all, a literary agent. I am sure he is pelted with manuscripts every week from people who fancy themselves writers but who don't have anything to say that hasn't been said. His response to my initial request to proofread it was guarded and skeptical. He told me to get a copy of "Stein on Writing" by Sol Stein, a legendary editor of best sellers. He told me to read the first half of the book and then complete a ten-point checklist he had sent me, for submittal. Driving home from our first meeting at my church, I was not the least bit disappointed. In fact I wanted him to be skeptical and hard to impress because I didn't want to be fooling myself into believing I was really onto something here if in fact I was really not a good writer. Several people had read the original manuscript and responded with much acclaim and enthusiasm, but they were friends of long standing and I was just a little suspicious of their objectivity. When this man got back to me in only two days and told me, I was actually on to something here and I should hone it to a point, I was excited. He had no reason whatsoever to encourage me at all if there was nothing to work with. I knew this, I also knew his reputation for total integrity, and character and that would preclude him stringing me along. He suggested I add to what I already had without removing anything at all. Okay, I liked hearing that. I was convinced this was very much a God authorized project and removing material wasn't on my radar. He told me to add to and expand on some more of the personal items. This I agreed with and so I sat down to write out an additional outline with more topics to discuss. I breezed through two pages of notebook paper in a few minutes and then, at the end of writing these new topics, I heard God's voice and I knew how this book would end. I heard God tell me to write this: "If you could go back in time and do this all again. Would you?" Not back before the divorce, changing that history was not an option because that was only half my decision. There were two wills involved in my divorce and I only had mine to surrender. No, God was asking me if I could go back in time to the day after the divorce…if God had grabbed me as I walked out of the courtroom in downtown Nashville December 1, 1999 and He said to me "Son, right now you can decide two paths. One will see you healed within maybe a year. You will remarry and have more children and there will be little sorrow. The good part is you won't hurt much but the bad part is you won't have much to give another hurting man. Alternatively, you can start over and go right down the path you took on day one. All the hurt, all the pain, every stumble, and every pitfall. You will grope in the same darkness and trip over the same obstacles. You will curse Me and come to hate Me, and you will be convinced I hate you. Then you will know my love for you like never before and you will be molded, shaped, tried, and refined until at the other end you are ready for me to use. If you had the option to choose either of these paths, would you do it all again?"

I wrote that down through tears, knowing I was going to have to think about that and finally answer it to complete this book. I didn't have to wait long to find my answer. About 3 days after writing that question down, I got a phone call from a long lost friend. Mike Rea had been a thoroughbred horse trainer for his entire life. I met Mike at church back home about 15 years ago and we had started a bible study together on the Delaware Park backside. It was a wonderful time of ministry. Mike and I were new Christians, just crazy enough to take God totally at His word without a lot of cynicism and we saw wonders happen and lives changed every day at the racetrack. Our friends Steve and Shelley Brown, Myra Carter, Joe Lewis Wallace, Pete, and a host of others, were just a bunch of Christian people who loved on others and saw them get saved.

I moved away and we fell out of touch…reconnecting now and again when I would go home. Two years ago, Mike had a tragic training accident. He was thrown form a horse he was galloping and sustained life threatening brain trauma. In the two years since, he had to learn to do everything again. He had to learn to walk, talk, drive a car, and take care of himself. To add to this dilemma, three weeks before our conversation, his wife of 15 years left him, taking his three children with her. I spent an hour on the phone with Mike. He was like a child, the words formed so slowly and he forgot many things we had done in the past. I could sense fear in his voice. He had already lost his ability to do the only thing he had every known to do for a living, and now he was losing his family as well. He was scared, angry, confused, and distraught. I heard myself relaying my own experiences with my divorce. I told him of the pain and the anger and the rotten things I screamed at God in the darkest night. I told him how betrayed I felt and how abandoned by God. Then I told him how wrong I was. How loved I was and how God had come to show me His love and mercy in ways I couldn't imagine. I told him that God is never taken by surprise by the events of our lives. I told him that God had a plan for the accident long before he had ever gotten aboard that horse that morning and God had a plan in place the morning Rochelle packed the kids and left. God always and only has our best interests at heart and if Mike would stay true to Him, regardless of what his eyes saw or his ears heard or his mind spoke, God would show him His grace. Then I told Mike this with tears in my eyes and my voice breaking... "Mike I went through 6 years of hell so that tonight I could minister to you. God allowed that pain because he knew even then that I would be talking to you tonight and you needed to hear that you could make it through this, and you needed to hear it from a guy who had been there. I can honestly say Mike, that looking back tonight I would go through it all again because you needed what I have for you tonight and I needed to suffer in order to have something to give. God is redeeming both of our situations tonight"

I meant that then and I mean it now. I don't know how many men, or women for that matter will read this book, but I do know God will use these words and these stories to heal some people. And that only came about through me enduring it. Only by His grace could I say I would walk through that valley again if it meant one person would be healed. I never thought I would be thankful for the pain and suffering I have endured, but now I can't imagine it any other way. I am someone new now because of where I have been and the path God had chosen for me to walk, and I am truly thankful for it. I know there are folks out there who need some of this medicine and I pray they get it as soon as they need it. I am limping from my wounds, but the limp draws attention to the battle that caused it, and that battle is my story of grace. I pray for every person who sees my victorious limp and wonders what caused it and how, and more importantly *who* got me through this. *Maybe that person is you*

I would be remiss if I left out the basic, obvious point of this book. My relationship with Jesus…fractured and imperfect as it was…is all that got me through my horrible nightmare. I wrote this from the perspective of my Christianity and assumed that most readers were Believers. But I began to realize that perhaps many men would find this book accidentally and have no knowledge or relationship with Jesus. So I wanted to introduce Him to those of you who have not met Him.

The relationship with Jesus is elemental to becoming complete as a man. You cannot become all that you were intended to be until you become one of His. How anyone can endure the pain of a marital failure without a rock of faith is beyond me. I have often remarked that I can understand the kind of pain that drives a man to harming his family and then himself in the midst of divorce, unless he knows God. Without some sort of faith base, I can easily see how that pain goes to the next horrible, tragic step. Jesus is who He claims He is. He is God's son, the savior of the world...the Savior of your soul, if you will allow Him. As Manning said, he is the Asker of the great question. Only by answering "yes" to Him do you receive His gift of eternal life. He died because He had to. Plain and simple. Without His death, our fate was sealed and we were doomed for hell. He died because we are not good enough to get to heaven on our own. He died because He loved us too much to leave us in that condition. All you need do in order to receive what He offers is say yes. "Yes I have sinned, yes I can't get there on my own, yes I know I need you, and yes I accept your gift of love. Yes, your death on the cross was actually intended for me, but You chose to take my place. Come into my heart, show me your limitless love for me, and give me the hope of glory." It's that simple. The changes take time but they start immediately. The best news is you don't have to face this hurt alone anymore. Let me make a few points about God, just in case you are wondering. He doesn't care that you are mad at Him…He knows. He doesn't care if you hate Him right now. He knows that too; don't bother trying to hide it. He didn't desire your divorce…this was not His best for you. But He is ready to make something indescribably beautiful out of the remnants and wreckage. He is ready to forgive your portion of this mess…all of it…even if it was entirely your fault. Even the parts where you responded to your wife's sins against you in a poor fashion. No matter what it is you did in your marriage, He loves you and wants to offer you forgiveness. He will never reject you. He is close to the brokenhearted and He bears our burdens and our hurts. He wants you to be happy again. Whether that means your marriage gets restored or you meet someone else or you find total contentment with just yourself and your children, I have no guarantee, but He wants you to be happy. He is there even when you don't think He is. He said, "Look, I am with you all the time and everywhere!" He loves your kids more than you do and doesn't want them to become statistics. He has some folks in mind who are part of His plan for your recovery. His plan is for them to find you on this dark path, come up beside you, and help you get through this. He has a plan to use your story to help someone else in pain. He is eagerly awaiting your prayer…Accepting Jesus is the first step toward healing.

If you already have accepted Him, and maybe all this pain and darkness has driven a wedge between you, remember two important things…

1: Only you moved…He never did.

2: He is still right there, as close as your next heartbeat and He misses your company as you miss your children. If you have never accepted Him, there is a model prayer in the Bible I would like to leave with you. You don't have to say it word for word, just speak your heart, and use this prayer as a model for saying you are sorry and asking God to begin His wonderful relationship with you… *"God, I ask for your mercy because I am a sinner. I haven't merely sinned…I am a sinner. Nevertheless, your word says you loved me so much that your son Jesus died on the cross to save me from myself, and from the punishment that my sins deserve. I believe He did that for me, I accept his gift of love and salvation. I give you my heart…just the way it is. Come in to my heart, make your home in me, and help me make my home in you. I let go of my sins, and I am reaching out to you right now. Save me, In Jesus name, Amen."* It's that simple. Your new life with Jesus has begun, my friend. The healing and forgiveness has begun too. Your Daddy loves you. If you are a believer, and a divorcee, and this book has opened up some old wounds or new ones. Maybe you are where I was for so long, embittered, distant, and angry at God and wondering if He truly loves you and if there is any way back to the relationship with Him you once knew and desired. Here is a model of the prayer I prayed many times on the road back home to him. In fact, I still pray this sometimes even now, when the pain creeps in or I miss my daughter. You see it isn't a journey with a destination. Except that, this takes us closer to Him. *"Father, I am hurting. I am so very hurting, lonely, and sad. I miss my child, and I miss having a wife. I am remembering my broken dreams tonight God, and it hurts. I know you promised to make all things new...tonight I need that desperately. Help me to rest in your promise and know you love me. Send your Holy Spirit to comfort me as you promised. I need you Lord. I am sorry I blamed you for things you had nothing to do with. I am sorry I am angry with you...I am sorry for hating you. Your love is hard to understand for a human...I believe you as much as I can, please help my unbelief. Pour your love on my wounded soul Father...please. I need you as the deer needs water after being pursued by the hunter. You are my hope and my rest. You are my Father. I need to rest in your arms daddy and lay my head on your shoulder. I am reaching out to you Father...please help me feel you reaching back and please heal my broken heart and bind up my wounds...just as you promised."* My prayers for you all are that you will come to know the amazing grace and love of your Father. His heart breaks for you just as yours does for your own children. There is no place more healing or restful than His presence. He is not mad at you, He misses you, and He loves you. Bring that heavy suitcase full of your broken pieces and dreams and the blurry, paint-smeared picture of life as you drew it out all those years ago. Let your Father make art out of it once again. Come drink your fill and find your rest.

www.ingramcontent.com/pod-product-compliance
Lightning Source LLC
LaVergne TN
LVHW051045080426
835508LV00019B/1722